GOOD THINGS

LOVE WATER

GOOD THINGS LOVE WATER

a collection of surf stories

by

CHRIS AHRENS

CHUBASCO PUBLISHING COMPANY

© *1994 by Chris Ahrens*
First Edition

Chubasco Publishing Company
P.O. Box 697
Cardiff by the Sea
California 92007


*Manufactured in the United States of America*

Cover painting and design by Michael Cassidy.


All rights reserved
ISBN 0-9640858-0-1  :  $14.95

*"Good things love water.  Bad things always been dry."*

John Steinbeck
*The Pastures of Heaven*

# CONTENTS

## READING INSTRUCTIONS

Get this book dirty. Take it to the beach, to Baja, or into the outback. Or, find a place that you loved as a kid. If you can't do that, go into your garage. The back seat of your car will do, or your bed, if it's full of sand. Do not, under any circumstances, put this book on the coffee table next to pretty volumes about "Napa's Wine Country." It is not to be read with shoes on, and you won't understand a word of it if your brain is being choked off by a tie. When you're finished reading, go out beyond the paved roads and mapped out surf camps, into the untamed world of surf. Surf hard.

—Chris Ahrens

## DEDICATION

To my daughter, Chrissy, and my wife, Tracy. And to my first surf partner, my brother, Dave. To Mom and Dad and Rick and Jackie. To everyone who ever gave me a wave, and to every English teacher who ever gave me a grade of F. To Chris O'Rourke, Steve Pinner, David Zerr, Tom Armor, Ron Elliot, and all the people I lived with, four in one bedroom. (Sorry for snoring and eating all your food.) To every surfer who took me in when I was penniless and wandering. Thanks, and God Bless you all.

## SPECIAL THANKS

Michael Cassidy, Pam Grubs, Don and Cheryl DeCandia, Dan Dunlop, Susan Lazear, Mark Lyon, Tom Wegener, Brett and Niki Haig, Shannon and Julie Daughty, Lyn O'Rourke and Jennifer Bird.

# A BELATED APOLOGY

*Phil Edwards is one of the greatest athletes of our century. He ranks highly among the best surfers of all times. In his prime he was like a predatory cat — so graceful — nearly undetectable at first. Then, he would impose his power over his grace and strike violently, moving loose and focused, never breaking stride. Power and grace. These were the pillars upon which his greatness rested. Power and grace and poetry and genius. But even great surfers have humble beginnings, and in Edwards' case, there are two lowly starting points — his first wave ridden at Oceanside pier in 1948 on a heavy, wooden, 14 foot lifeguard board. And his first trip to Hawaii four years later.*

Phil Edwards was 15 years old, and unknown outside of the little group he surfed with who regarded him highly for his ground-breaking techniques in performance surfing. Now he stood alone literally, a ruddy young boy with a boarding pass, clutching his sack lunch, and only half listening to his mother's warning, "If you're not back in three weeks I'm coming to get you." With that, Phil kissed his mom and boarded the prop-plane to Honolulu, Hawaii.

In the Islands the kid happened upon a surfer headed for Makaha, and begged a ride from the man whom he recognized as Pat Curren. The man didn't recognize the kid, but agreed to take him along with him. As they drove, Curren was silent, never initiating conversation, and speaking only to answer Phil's many questions with a simple yes or no. Phil watched the beautiful desolation intensify until he was faced with tiny waves breaking on a clear-water point. Curren sat silently in the car without moving. This was not enough for a big-wave man like him, and he dropped the kid on the side of the road. Phil watched the smoking car retrace its tracks as Curren headed out to the North Shore.

A handful of small wooden homes occupied by protective locals were clustered near the point. Beyond that there was nothing. The kid found himself all alone at the end of the earth. He was stoked.

Phil hid his suitcase in the bushes and, with nowhere else to go, he paddled out to get wet. As the tide dropped, bigger waves began to show on the reef. Some of the local surfers paddled out to join him, giving him the greeting "Hey kid, stay off of the waves."

But the kid surfed well, better than any young haole they had ever seen, and he quickly earned enough admiration to be allowed to surf there without hassle. He found the warm water to his liking, and, as the small waves increased in size, he noticed that they produced more power than anything back home. His board became loser. It turned effortlessly beneath his feet. Running to the nose he held trim, and moved quickly through to the shorebreak for a standing island pullout, or the momentary weightlessness produced by colliding with the backwash.

Phil stayed out for hours in the now head-high surf, and played little games with the bouncy shorebreak. Like all good surf sessions this one did it's job by helping him to forget his troubles, in this case that he had no place to stay.

But the kid did not think about accommodations when he left the surf. He was absorbing paradise—the feeling of being washed by the salty clear water, and the blowing of the warm wind which caused salt crystals to form nearly instantly on his skin and eyelashes. He looked up at the steep mountains and back to the fun surf, and he wondered what types of waves lay in either direction of the point. The possibilities were endless. It was at that moment that he fell deeply and forever in love with Hawaii.

Within minutes the necessities of life began to weigh upon him. He sat in the sand with the cardboard suitcase, and the balsa board that he had made in his garage. The sun was getting low when he first wondered where he would spend the night. He ate the remainder of the lunch his mom had packed for him, and scanned the area, noting good possibilities for shelter in a small clump of bushes near the point. He had resolved himself to sleeping in the bushes when a beaten up '36 Ford rolled up with a large stocky man at the wheel, and a passenger hanging half way outside of the car window.

Makaha was a tightly knit community in those days where everyone knew each other. The sight of any haole, especially a young boy with a surfboard and a suitcase, was so unusual that the men had to pull over to check it out. The driver looked directly at the kid and then chuckled slightly before Phil recognized that it was his old friend, Walter Hoffman. The other man, who was built like a wild animal, was named Buzzy. Trent. The boy had heard the lifeguards from home say that he was one of the best big-wave riders in Hawaii, a man who had pioneered big surf at Makaha and on the North Shore.

Once he realized the boy's homeless situation, Hoffman picked up the suitcase and threw it into the car. Trent helped the kid put the board into the trunk. On the way home, Trent spoke excitedly about a new swell that was about to hit the island. Then, without warning, Hoffman pulled over to the side of the road and asked the kid to sit in the driver's seat. "Do you know how to drive?" he asked.

"No," said Phil.

"Well it's easy," said Hoffman, as he illustrated the use of the clutch, gears and brakes.

Phil did find driving easy, and after a few near misses with palm trees and houses, he knew enough to become a surfer's chauffeur. He was directed down old dirt roads and up dead-end streets, and then up a winding road, and up over an overgrown path until they arrived at an abandoned army instillation, an old semicylindrical metal shelter which Phil later learned was called a Quonset hut.

The land near the shelter was completely wild and overgrown. Nailed up near the door were the dried fins of big fish that had been speared and eaten by the men, and cooked over the much-used rock pit near the door. Inside, the place was sparse but roomy. Walter introduced the kid to another man, Leslie Williams.

That night after a dinner of fish which Buzzy had speared, rice, and sweet pineapples stolen from the fields, the kid lay on an old army cot thinking, "In one day I went from having nothing, to having a great place to stay with some great guys." He went to sleep smiling.

The next morning he awoke early with a warm wind that came through the mountains, and whistled through the gaps in the tin roof. He had slept so soundly that he nearly forgot where he was, but he sat up quickly with the remembrance of his luck. Outside everything was green and alive. He breathed deep and took in the burden of the beauty of Hawaii. The crew were soon up too, and Buzzy spoke in a staccato voice, wringing his hands and saying "Maybe Sunset today. Maybe Sunset today." The thought of big surf at Sunset Beach seemed to make Buzzy extremely happy. The boys loaded up the boards, piled into the Ford, and relaxed as Phil drove to Makaha Point without mishap. The waves were good, a solid four to six foot with nobody out. Phil parked the car, jumped out and reached for his board, but was told to get back behind the wheel. They were going to the North Shore, more precisely, Sunset Beach.

The kid tried to concentrate on the new sensation of driving, but the abundant greenery, and thoughts of North Shore waves distracted him as he rolled up over the mountains. He wondered about the size of the surf. Were the waves really as big as ten-story buildings, and did they fall on you like an avalanche? Buzzy spoke joyfully about the surf, saying that he (Phil) had better not go out if it was too big. Walter agreed seriously. The kid didn't say anything. He just drove silently, remembering the time when he was 13 years old, and was criticized by the older guys for fading in toward the whitewater on a big wave at Dana Point. The words "Head for the green," echoed in his head as Phil drove and smiled slightly, confidently, at the memory. On that day he had introduced the older surfers to performance surfing—fading, and turning and riding near the curl in a way that the men on hand at Dana Point that day had not dreamed of. He was older now, and a better surfer, and today he would again show the older generation something new.

The men in the car discussed their equipment, and found general agreement that Curren made some of the best big-wave guns in the islands. "Yeah, I love his boards," said Trent "but he's so damned quiet that I never know what he's thinking. You know how he is, sitting outside at Sunset without saying a word and then, when you think he's nearly asleep, he'll catch the biggest wave of the day." There was admiration in Trent's voice as he spoke of Curren.

Coming out of miles of pineapple fields, Phil saw the North Shore for the first time—a powder-blue sky dotted by white clouds, and surf breaking for as far as he could see. It looked small to him, and he was surprised by the reactions of the other surfers. "Floor it," said Walter before Phil hit the gas.

"Let's go, let's go," said Buzzy nearly frantically. The kid drove down the thin highway, past small tin-roofed homes and well-kept fields, some of which were being cultivated by men using nothing but a plow pulled by an ox. They drove past miles of empty surf, perfect waves fanned by offshore winds formed symmetrical, blue triangles. Phil was directed to pull over at a beautiful bay called Waimea, where they watched waves cap near the rock point and then break in deep water. Trent spoke about the massive waves that broke there at times, saying that they were impossible to ride and would beat you to the bottom every time.

They drove past fun surf, and past a spot they called the Banzai Pipeline, where another perfect but unrideable wave broke in pipe formation in shallow water over coral spikes. They continued to drive without seeing another surfer anywhere until Phil was told to pull over onto the shoulder. Here they faced a long, wide beach.

The kid looked out and watched a clean wave of about four foot break fairly close to shore. He thought, "This looks like home; I like this."

Walter and Leslie got out of the car and grabbed their boards. Buzzy gave a loud hoot, and stood next to the kid, and said with serious joy, "Look at that, man, look at it!" Phil followed Buzzy's eyes far away past the medium-sized surf of the shorebreak he was watching, to a place on the edge of a massive rip, where a huge peak toppled in slow motion.

Seeing that Walter and Leslie were already on their way out, Buzzy grabbed his board and ran to catch them, outdistancing them as he committed himself to the river of a rip, and then paddling over to the big peak.

The wave was blown clean by the strong offshore wind as Buzzy dropped into it without hesitation. Phil could see that the wave was not only bigger than he had imagined, but it jacked up and up and up, until it was vertical, and powerful—the biggest, most powerful wave that he had ever seen.

Buzzy rode with forward aggression, in a style that suggested total dominance. But even his massive frame looked frail against the sea that day.

Leslie and Walter were soon in the peak also, and each of them caught waves in their turn, performing with skill and courage. Phil grabbed his board, and fearing to look toward the sea, he paddled out with his head down. The rip was fast and no waves broke in or near it. He drifted near an inside wave where the terrible power tore a solid hole over the reef.

This was the area that Buzzy had warned against being caught in. The kid paddled hard for the outside where the others were sitting, looking like dots. He could see that this was a survival situation.

Phil sat in the pack with the others and

looked around for the mushy peak he had seen from shore. A wave approached quickly and Phil spun around and knee-paddled for it, just as he had always done in California. The strong offshore wind blew him back over the top and out of the wave as drops of warm water pelted his skin. Walter looked with concern at Phil and told him not to knee-paddle into the waves saying that if he did, he would never make the drop. Phil dropped from his knees and laid flat onto his board and scanned the horizon for sets.

Not even Buzzy seemed calm now. They all huddled, waiting quietly for a long time until the next wave approached, a beautiful peak, a gift to the kid who began to stroke in early from a prone position. The others watched protectively as the small boy paddled down. The wave picked the boy up, and pulled him back up to the lip. The boy paddled down again, and again, and each time the water rushing up the face took him to the top. He paddled now with all of his strength, fighting the wind and the spray which rendered him temporarily blind. He moved down the face, into the guts of the wave. He could feel that the situation was critical now, but he took two extra strokes, just as he had been instructed. Then he stood up, feeling the weightlessness of the drop as adrenaline kicked in. He saw the men's blurred and concerned faces watching with appreciation from the channel. The wave unloaded, it's power building as he skipped down the face. Once at the bottom of the wave he relaxed, nursed a turn, and rode to the shoulder where he bounced out and over the top.

Having survived the first wave, he felt better. He rode half a dozen others, not in the perfect manner he would become known for, but good enough to prove to himself and to the men that he could surf the North Shore.

Phil was the first to paddle in, and he watched the men get spectacular rides and terrible wipeouts in the giant surf. Sometimes all of them took off on the same wave together. Eventually they all made shore and sat together on the sand for a while, verbally replaying their rides.

Buzzy spoke for them all saying, "Hey, did you see Phil out there today?" Hoffman smiled proudly. Buzzy gave the kid a warm slap on the shoulder.

Phil felt very grown up as he drove the men to the restaurant in Haleiwa. After lunch they decided to check out the surf at Haleiwa. The waves looked clean and fun, similar to ones Phil had ridden in Dana Point. This was his chance to show the others what he could do. He paddled out quickly without fully assessing the conditions, and with the intention of showing off.

After paddling out the kid discovered that he was wrong again. The waves were not at all like the ones he had ridden at home, but walled up, steep and critical, moving massive amounts of water quickly to shore. He let a few waves pass beneath him, and watched them explode as they hit the reef. They broke like a concrete sidewalk in an earthquake, and he knew that he must be careful to pick a clean one. He paddled down into a set wave and began to drop. Moving below the angry ledge, dropping, falling through the air, hanging on, reconnecting, falling some more, he somehow survived. Unlike Sunset, the worst was not over after the drop, however, and he looked out to see the wall stretching down and away from him. The wave found sufficient depth to break, and broke hard, causing the kid and his board to fly in separate directions.

After being held down in the darkness, Phil came up gasping and pushing back the thick foam. Another wave was upon him now, and he dove down deep, back into darkness. He came up and faced a third wave, and a fourth, and found that he was being pulled out to sea and down the beach.

On the beach the men watched as the boy tried to swim against the powerful rip. They knew that it was hopeless and so they asked one of their Hawaiian friends to go out and rescue him. Phil felt a little smaller as he drove back to Makaha.

What followed were some of the best days in the kid's life. Each day was filled with fun surf at Makaha, or big waves on the North Shore.

After many winters of Hawaiian waves, Phil Edwards became a master of large surf, and especially excelled in the six to twelve foot range. He rode huge Himalayas alone, and became so confident at Sunset that he would sometimes jump into the face of the wave at the last second, and take the ride to the bottom, freefalling, for the fun of it, without his board. He became the first surfer ever to ride Banzai Pipeline. The tail end of that historic wave was photographed by Bruce Brown. Quietly he developed his massive natural ability until he was generally considered the best surfer in the world, an honor that he wore with dignity.

Other surfers, too, distinguished them-selves on big days in Hawaii. Pat Curren, the man he had met on his first trip to Hawaii, was one of them. Pat built advanced boards and rode some huge waves on them, walking away after-ward without a word. But Curren remained an enigma to Edwards and nearly everyone else who knew him.

Buzzy eventually did ride Waimea, and took on some of the biggest waves ever ridden there. And there was Greg Noll, Mike Stange, and George Downing, someone who Edwards regards as the best big-wave rider of his day. The years passed and the surfing changed, but Edwards and Hoffman remained close friends.

A few years ago Phil accompanied Walter to Hoffman's home in Cabo San Lucas. One evening Phil found himself alone at the Hoffman compound when Pat Curren, a man he had known and surfed with for nearly four decades, knocked at the door. Curren had not changed his mysterious manner a bit, and Edwards found himself trying to stimulate conversation while Pat sat silently. After one particularly long silence Curren took a pull on his beer and said, "The kid's doing pretty good."

Edwards chuckled to himself at the understatement concerning Curren's son, former World Champion, Tom Curren. Again there was silence until Pat looked to Phil and said sincerely, "Hey, I didn't know who you were."

"I wasn't anybody," replied Edwards.

It was nearly an apology, and it took 40 years to get there, but coming from Pat Curren, it was worth the wait.

$$*$$

*Phil Edwards continues to surf and build classic surfboards in Capistrano Beach, California where he lives with his wife, Mary.*

# THE LEGEND OF DAVE PEPPER

*In 1972 , I met a 16 year-old surfer at a surf spot called Angourie in New South Wales, Australia. His name was Dave Pepper, and he was the best surfer in the water for three days running. More impressive than his surfing ability, however, was the way he lived. Like a wise and wild animal, he moved through the continent of his birth, leaving nothing but his tracks. The day I met him he had just finished hiking 50 miles of coast, which was inaccessible by car. There he had discovered what he called "good, virgin waves."*

*He had taken nothing with him for his journey except his surfboard and his backpack, which contained fishhooks, sinkers, and monofilament line. Now he was headed back to Sydney to settle things with the alcoholic father who had beaten him up and kicked him out. One night we cooked fish that he had caught, over a wood fire. He impressed me with his knowledge of the ocean and the bush. One morning I awoke with the sun, and he was gone without a trace.*

*In 1989 I returned to Australia. There I ran into a friend named Steve at the Bondi Post Office. After catching up on old times, I asked Steve if he knew of Dave Pepper. He not only knew him, he had traveled with him once. Steve told me the following tale.*

Nobody paid much attention to Dave when he drove through Surfer's Paradise, the Waikiki pop-out surf ghetto in Queensland—nobody but the cops, who didn't like his rig much. To them it was a bundle of revenue, a rolling pile of red dirt over a rust and duct taped combi. They issued him a stack of citations and let him go.

The make-up and silicone queens were less attentive. The old hat, worn jeans, and once plain white, now mud-smeared T-shirt, indicated an empty wallet, and no fashion sense. But Dave didn't give a stuff; he was going into the deep north, as far as his trusty combi would take him.

I was hitching up to Noosa Heads from the Gold Coast when he picked me up. I hadn't seen him for a while, and he seemed neither happy or sad to see me. Without a word he pulled over and I stashed my gear into the van. Then he asked me to toss the citations in the rubbish bin that was located near my door. I threw them away, he smiled, and we moved on.

Dave died a little inside when he saw that the farmhouse he had once lived on in Noosa was gone. The trees and meadows where there had been koalas and kangaroos had been flattened by bulldozers. Angry crowds fought their way past the dry condos to get to the two-foot point waves. I asked him if I could travel with him further up the coast and he said that would be okay.

He didn't say much, and I don't think he smiled again until we were 200 miles north of there. It was another 300 miles before he began to laugh. Then we hit Cairns and he was tight again. Miles from there we picked up an aboriginal man hitching. The man had a distant look in his eyes, and after we dropped him off Dave told me that they had destroyed his soul when they poisoned his land.

Dave swore me to secrecy, telling one of his few jokes by saying that there was a tentative contract out on my life, to be fulfilled if anyone found out about the place he was taking me. I think he was joking, anyway. He told me to reach into the glove box, and pull out a photo. The photo was an out of focus shot of the wave that I live to get back to. He's not really too worried that I'd tell anyone, however, most of the surfers from the south would crack before they got through the desert. And if I told, he would hurt me really bad, as bad as my infraction would hurt him.

*Steve digressed a bit, as a dreamy look came over him, and he smiled distantly before giving me a little background on his friend.*

Dave Pepper. Big Wave Dave, we called him. I first heard of him in the late '70s, when the rumor was that he was the most gifted surfer in Sydney. He was a natural, the best surfer by miles at every break he rode. But he never cared about surf stardom. When photographers tried to shoot him, he'd paddle in. When people tried to sponsor him, he turned them down. He would sometimes surf in a contest area, catch one wave, get tubed and paddle in before anyone knew who he was. Mostly he got as far from Sydney as he could, hitching into the bush every weekend from the time he could carry a surfboard. He never drank or smoked or hung out with his mates much. He had an aboriginal girlfriend from Redfern. Some of the boys used to pay him out, behind his back of course, about that.

He earned his reputation and his name "Big Wave Dave" by riding the Fairy Bower. He always had the worst boards, and rode the biggest waves. He often paddled out before sunrise. No matter how big it got, he was there, even if he got hurt, and he got hurt a lot. I saw him hit the rock once when I was paddling out. His head was opened up and blood poured from it. I was a lot older than him, and I told him to go in. He did, but only for a moment. In his car, he had some duct tape which he put over the gash. Then he paddled back out, got really deep and hit the rock again. He stayed out until dark that night, getting the biggest waves from the deepest position.

Another time, a biker on the boardwalk poured beer down his girlfriends bathing suit bottoms. Dave tackled the guy onto the concrete and then smacked him senseless. We were all too afraid to move because this guy had some pretty tough mates. These were heavy guys, guys who might kill you if you got 'em too pissed off. But Dave held his own for a while with four or five of them until they finally got him down and kicked him silly. He looked terrible, all cut and swollen. But he just kept getting up and coming at them. God, it was ugly, the way they beat him. But that's Dave. If he thinks he's right, he'll go to his grave fighting. I don't know if he felt humiliated by the beating or betrayed by his mates, but he didn't come around much after that.

I didn't see him for a long time, but I heard about him. Everywhere I traveled, from Byron Bay, to Bells Beach, to Western Australia, I heard about this crazy guy on a beat up board who took off deeper than anyone, and then disappeared before anyone could talk to him. I knew it was Dave.

He was in his early-20s the last time I saw him, but his face was wrinkled and scarred. His eyes were deep, thin slits that reflected only an occasional flash of light blue. He was tall for a surfer, about 6'2", thin, but rock solid, and he had a glare that could knock you down.

*Steve picked up the thread of the story*

*again and continued telling about his wanderings with Dave in The Northern Territories.*

As we got further into the reef there were bright blue bays and coves where he would sometimes stop, take out his spear and return with a big snapper or a small shark that he cooked over a wood fire. Once in a while he would hunt the land with his spear, and return with a rabbit that he cooked in red clay, a method taught to him by his abo friends. The only time I could get him to talk was when he was having a drink with me. Because he never drank, it only took one to get him going. He was usually given to a few words, but he could get jawing sometimes for hours over a bottle of port.

He liked to talk about the land, about the aborigines, about fishing, about big waves, and deserted islands, and his aboriginal girlfriend.

We drove through rain forests, and around swamps, through the deserts and into an aborigine reserve where he knew most of the people. He stopped and gave them a few fish. They gave him witchety grubs, and pieces of anthill, both of which he ate joyfully before offering some to me. I was unable to stomach the wild food and declined, which made him laugh as he ate my share. He said that the food tasted clean and healthy.

We slept in the open that night. I had no idea which stars I was looking at, but they were bright and close to the earth.

The next day we crossed a bridge as the rains came. Later we heard that the bridge had washed out behind us during that storm. It happened every few years. Everybody in the area had boats, so it didn't matter to them. Dave rented a boat that we took to a small island. He paid the rent on the boat by giving its owner a big fish.

I swear, Dave could have been king of that island. The black people, I think they were from New Guinea, spoke English, but not with an Australian accent. They pronounced his name Div. It sounded funny. We laughed, and they laughed, and then they would break into a language that Dave seemed to be learning, and they all laughed some more. They showed us the ultimate respect and kindness and offered food— mostly mangoes and fish.

I was getting hungry to surf, and I saw no waves. Dave had not answered one of my questions about surf for 300 miles, and he was getting on my nerves. I started thinking that he was as crazy as some of the stories about him suggested. We slept in a thatched hut that night, if you can call it sleeping. The mosquitoes all went for me. Dave, like the islanders, was somehow exempt.

In the morning we ate wild fruits, goanna, and part of an emu egg. I'd had enough of the primitive culture and wanted to go surfing. Dave and his friends just sat and ate and laughed and talked for hours. I was sweating and anxious when some of the men got up and asked us to follow them. They showed us to a wooden canoe.

We loaded our boards, drinking water, dive gear, a heavy duty wooden spear which Dave had made, and a rifle onto the canoe. It barely held us, and I wondered if we would make it. Dave just put a primitive paddle into my hands without saying anything, implying that I start paddling. The little windswells nearly capsized us many times. We paddled for a very small-looking island, maybe a half mile away.

Once, thinking that the boat was about to sink, I looked back and saw Dave smiling gleefully. I had never before seen him so happy.

The island must have been a lot further than it looked because it took us hours to get there.

You think you've seen the perfect wave? You haven't. It is impossible to describe this color of blue. And how do you show speed, or the way that just the right amount of wind blew offshore. Thin, fast, and hollow, with a long curl line, the wave peeled without section for 300 yards, maybe more. Down to nothing. Dave paddled out, right into the peak as soon as he put the boat ashore and tied it down in a rocky cove. The water was so clear there. Small fish broke the surface as I put my feet into the water. The island was a thick mat of green, and, as far as I could tell, completely uninhabited.

The waves broke in long tapering walls, sucking off the reef. Out the back it was big, triple overhead and bigger. Dave was late on each drop, and turned hard just as the power unloaded inches behind him. Then he would take the highest line possible and disappear in the curl. When he outran the section, he would pull over the top as the rest of the wave went unridden for 200-plus yards. I never did see him cutback the entire time, and I never saw him fall, something that would have been disastrous because the reef was sharp and shallow and he never wore a legrope.

It looked extremely dangerous, and there were no hospitals for hundreds of miles. I contented myself to ride the inside—a little overhead, fast, warm, and perfect. I've never ridden better waves anywhere in my life.

After many hours my arms ached, and Dave paddled in and up to me. He didn't bother to take off on the waves there, even though they were perfect. He had his fill of surf, and he had an amazingly clear look in his eyes, a look that explorers probably had when they first saw Australia. Or a look that the first surfers would have worn. It was a timeless look, like the rocks and the sea, and the fish. He belonged to this place.

We didn't speak, but I understood what he was feeling, and we laughed hard. I followed his lead back to the boat. On shore he changed into his pants and boots, took his rifle from the boat, sternly looked at me and said simply "Beware of blacksnakes and crocodiles." Then he walked into the thick bush.

I took a big stick from the ground, and got back into the boat, nearly too scared to move. Dave couldn't have been far off because I could hear him sloshing through the muddy water. Then I heard the repeated sounds of his rifle followed by rustling in the bushes, and a series of deep thuds. He returned a while later dragging a bleeding croc which was still thrashing a little. The thing was about five feet long, and its mouth was wired shut. It still had not quit moving when, without a word, Dave clubbed the thing on the head. It made me sick the way the animal kept jerking around on the ground, but Dave unflinchingly cut it open and threw the guts into the sea. Then he went to his knees and thanked the animal for its life. He wrapped the dead body in leaves. Noting my concern, he assured me that the aborigines would use every part of the croc.

I lit a fire and we cooked the fish on a stick over it. We spent the afternoon on the little island and surfed the long right. Dave left many of our supplies and our water on the island in order to compensate for the increase in cargo. Our trip back was even more difficult than our approach had been, but we made it to shore without losing any of our gear.

When we returned to the mainland the islanders were glad to see the crocodile. Dave gave it to them along with the fish. In return they gave us mangoes, and a place to stay, probably forever.

At my request, Dave drove me back to Cairns where I got a bus to Sydney. He didn't try to talk me into staying, nor did he lecture me on the stupidity of my return to the city. He simply took me to the bus station, shook my hand and said, "There are a few more places I want to check out before the magazines get at them." Then he retraced his tracks, no doubt back to the island, and beyond.

He dropped me a card once, and it just said "Surf's great. Life's perfect."

*With that Steve ceased speaking, and he stared straight ahead. And then, as if he were offering a toast, he lifted his eyes and said, "Good luck Dave Pepper. May they never find you."*

✶

# ONE TO NOTHING

Kingsley "Knackers" Kernovski is a good surfer and a good bloke. Originally from Australia, he made his reputation by surfing, shaping, and living freely. Like most Australian surfers, he has sacrificed his life to chasing good Australian waves in bad Australian cars.

Once he owned a Holden that he absolutely loathed. It wasn't the Holden's fault, really, Knackers never took care of the thing, punished it for its sins—ran it without oil, never gave it a tune up, and drove it literally into the ground where it lay parked on the dirt road that led to his house in Noosa Heads.

One morning he got into the car and tried to start it. Nothing. In his fury he ran into the house and pulled a shotgun from the wall rack. Running back outside he gave the car both barrels at point blank. It felt good, so he loaded up again and blasted the tires. Then he blew out the windshield. Blasting out the radiator was especially satisfying. His roommate heard the sound of gunfire and ran out to see what was going on now. "You're mad, mate," said the roommate in reference to Kingsley's violent attack.

"No, I'm not," retorted Kernovski. "Give it a go." With that, Kingsley handed the rifle to the roommate who soon entered into the joy of splattering glass as he destroyed the one remaining window. Then the roommate blasted the grill. "Hey, that does feel good," he said with a smile. "Can I borrow your rifle for a moment?"

Kingsley graciously allowed his mate to use the shotgun, and his mate ran into the frontyard and blasted his own car for a while.

When he returned to the backyard he saw Kingsley standing over the dead Holden, kicking in the fenders, and wearing a satisfied smile. "Now," said Kingsley, "I'm going to drive the car to work in the morning."

"There's no way," said his mate, looking at the battered heap. "You won't even get the thing started."

"I'll bet you a hundred bucks that I drive it to work in the morning," said Knackers.

"Okay, you're on," said his mate, and they shook on it.

The next morning Kingsley, who was then a D-9 Caterpillar operator, got into the big machine, started it up, and drove it directly into his car. There he began to push the Holden down the dirt and gravel road. It flipped over and Kingsley backed up and raced toward the car again. It flipped a couple of more times and began to roll down the hill toward work. Kingsley got a good run at the car and pushed it further down the road. He wounded and mashed and rolled the beast for over a mile until it lay in front of the work yard as nothing more than a compact metal ball.

Another D-9 operator pulled up in his car, looked over at the metallic ball, and ran to his machine. Kingsley pushed the metal ball into the middle of the large field and backed up. The other operator sat in his machine on the opposite side of the field, and said, "Go." Then the two of them proceeded to play soccer (Australian Rules of course), using the car as the ball, until driver number two got past Kingsley and rolled the metallic hunk down a steep cliff, thus winning the game by scoring the only possible goal that day.

∗

# THE PASSAGE

*For most gremmies the process from the shorebreak of childhood into the outside and adult life is a gradual one. Time is marked by fun, fear, and tortures inflicted by peers, enemies, and heroes. The severe poundings of man and sea shatter or steady them. The idols of youth will become friends, remain larger-than-life icons, or be seen for the ruthless scoundrels they sometimes were. Regardless, a new identity will emerge from a gremmie's ruins. It's not an easy passage. For every wave decently ridden, there will be a thousand seemingly fatal wipeouts. For every joke told by you, there will be two told about you. You will be humiliated beyond measure and the glory you hoped for will come slowly if it ever comes at all.*

*Nobody's really sure just how it happens. There is no official test to pass. But all at once you find that you are no longer a grem. You're a surfer, and you will be a surfer from then on. For my brother Dave and I the passage from gremmie to real surfer took only a few minutes on a windblown afternoon in December of 1963.*

They called us gremmies, and treated us like crap. To real surfers we were unwanted pests, something to lock in the trunk, tie to the surf racks, and onto pier pilings in boxer shorts where we were baptized in chocolate milk and corn flakes. We were forced to eat sand, and run around the beach on all-fours, barking like dogs. Once they shaved my head into a crude Mohawk and painted stripes all over it.

Not only were we gremmies, we were twice cursed by being inlanders. Fathered by a

27

former Santa Monica surfer, who from necessity had turned away from the sea and settled in the low-rider capitol of the world, East Los Angeles, Dad understood our need to get out of that smog pit and ride waves once in a while.   So, each weekend he loaded up the station wagon with friends and surfboards, and transported us en masse to Malibu, Huntington, Doheny, or Swami's.

One Saturday Dad was busy, and all the surfers in our town old enough to drive claimed to have full cars.  It felt like surf on that crisp sunny morning, and I had that sickness you get when you know it's good, but can't get to it.

There was a system in those days that worked like this—surfers with cars would drive around town looking for surfers without cars who had gas money.  Sometimes the two groups didn't know each other, but when a surfer with a car found a surfer with gas money, he made him an offer to get him to the beach.  In this, the time of 25 cent gas, it usually cost the rider about 50 cents.

The familiar-looking, lowered, cherry-red woody belched smoke all over Whittier Boulevard before it came to a stop, spewing oil onto our driveway.  That car seemed as out of place there as the big, blond surfer who lumbered from it in his Greg Noll T-shirt, black Converse tennis shoes, and white Levis.  His name was Sam, and he walked up to the front door, and talked Mom into letting us go to the beach with him.  "Yes ma'am, we certainly will be going to church first," he assured her.  I had never spoken to Sam before, but he was well-known in our town as "Big Sam," a nickname, we were told, he picked up along with a tattoo of a dagger in San Quenton

State Prison.

I recognized some of the other guys in the woody also. There was Mickey The Dog, and Frenchfry Dave, and Stinky Thompson, a guy who was holding up liquor stores when I was earning Cub Scout merit badges. It didn't matter who we went with, however, we were going surfing.

All Mom saw was the polite veneer of a man with a sincere smile. She handed Samuel, as he called himself, three dollars for gas, packed him an extra sandwich, and kissed Dave and I good-bye.

Pressing church pants against paraffin wax seemed somehow sacrilegious. But we loaded up our boards, and squeezed into a tiny crawl space below them. There, behind a thick veil of cigarette smoke sat four of the city's heaviest juvenile offenders. Frenchfry, Stinky, and Dog stared at us as we piled into the car, where, beyond the tinted windows, they were dealing out cards along with a pimply faced, rail-thin kid with a greasy, brown pompadour, starched bell bottoms and a sweat-stained white undershirt. They called him "Birdie," and he seemed to be the leader of these Post Office celebrities.

At first I was fearful, but I began to relax as we drove, thinking that these were pretty cool guys, and that we could hold our own against them if any of them moved against me or Dave.

We chugged north with the throttle to the floor at 45 miles-per hour—destination, Lunada Bay, a place whose name inspired fear in both Dave and I. Lunada was famous for big waves, and neither of us had ever ridden anything over four feet.

Things were quiet until Birdie flicked a cigarette butt at Dog, the bottle-blond surfer wearing the iron cross and army jacket. Dog, who had sulked silently behind me until then, now sprang to life in response to the insult. Dog dove over me, kicking me in the head as he clawed at Birdie. The cigarette smouldered, and then set the grass matt beneath us aflame. I put out the fire with my towel, and settled in to enjoy the fight. We hooted as they tore at each other and rattled the boards above us.

Everything was going great until the woody slammed to a halt, and boards and bodies compressed into one solid mass near the front seat. Looking out the window, I could see that we were in a Safeway parking lot, somewhere in West L.A.

Big Sam turned around and demanded more gas money. We all shut up at the same time. Birdie let Dog go from the headlock he had him in, and fished in his pockets until he came up with a quarter. That did it. Sam slammed his big fist into the door, and with an intensity that made you feel he was looking only at you, he asked for more money. Everyone dug deep. Nothing.

Then Sam threw Dave a comb and told him to look good. Dave had that innocent altar boy look that parents always fell for, and Sam was counting on it to make him some money. He gave Dave instructions on getting money from people, saying, "Walk up smiling to any old woman you see, and tell her that your father has run out of gas. Make sure that you ask her only for a nickel or a dime, no more." Dave refused to cooperate, saying that it was dishonest. Birdie whipped him across the face with a cord made of licorice laces. I told him to knock it off, but got whipped by the cord repeatedly until Big Sam restrained the punk's arm. I shrugged my shoulders at Dave, and he combed his hair and went off in search of gas money.

Minutes later Dave returned with eight bucks and some change. Sam grabbed all of the money without so much as a "thank you," and walked into Safeway, returning with big jars of peanut butter and jelly, Wonder Bread, and two, one-gallon bottles of Red Mountain Wine. Sam filled the tank and pulled back onto the freeway, drinking from the jug, and passing it into the hole where we all sat huddled together. I took a sip. It tasted terrible, but I pretended to like it.

A light fog hung over the rocky cove at Lunada Bay, and the waves made a dull, sick sound as they pounded the cliff and blew spray onto the freighter that lay broken in two at the point. We couldn't tell how big the surf was outside, but we were sure that it was too big for us. We hoped that Sam would want to go someplace else to surf, maybe Rincon.

The second bottle was opened, and the group walked out of the car and onto the dirt above the cliff. Dog took a long pull before walking out onto a drainpipe where he did a spinner 100 feet above the rocks. We sat and laughed with the rest of the boys, but Big Sam scowled at us, jerked our boards from the wagon and pitched them over the cliff.

They all roared with laughter as Dave and I scampered down the thin dirt and rock trail after our boards while being chased by rocks and bottles. We found our boards at the bottom of the cliff near the water. They were in one piece, but badly scratched and dinged.

There were good four-foot waves breaking inside of the cove when Dave and I decided to paddle out. The surfers on the cliff had big reputations in our town as being hot surfers, and we, not being hot surfers ourselves, were nervous about riding in front of them. Eventually the others descended the cliff. We figured that the waves were not good enough for them because nobody paddled out except for Birdie and Dog. They made their way clumsily to the shorebreak where Dave and I were surfing alone.

There they struggled to maintain balance, and they nearly lost their boards just trying to sit on them. Dave and I looked at each other. These guys were kooks! Still, they kept taking off in front of us, loosing their boards into the rocks. After about 15 minutes, they returned to the beach.

Spending nearly an hour in the cold water without a wetsuit, Dave and I agreed to paddle in to warm ourselves next to the raging beach fire which somebody had started. The others crammed sloppily made peanut butter and jelly sandwiches into their mouths followed by swigs of Red Mountain. They did not bother us then, and I figured that they were going to leave us alone for a while.

They didn't say anything, but giggled among themselves as we warmed up by the fire in our wet trunks and searched the rocks for our clothes and towels. Then, as I looked closely into the flames, I caught a final glimpse of my pants being turned to ash in the burning driftwood. "My clothes!" I shouted in disbelief, desperately reaching to the flames before being repelled by the great heat. When I turned to the others, they were howling with laughter. Dave's clothes had been burnt in the fire with mine. I was mad, but there was nothing that I could do. So, with no place else to go, Dave followed me back into the water. He was just a little kid, and being afraid he might start crying I told him to shut up, even though he wasn't saying anything. "Mom's going to kill us," he sobbed.

"Shut up," I said again.

We were the only ones out in all of Lunada Bay as the fog lifted revealing the threat of the point. Lumpy and big onshore lines poured in from the outside. To us it looked like the biggest surf in the world at Waimea Bay.

The others sat drinking on the beach, breaking glass on the rocks while we rode the shorebreak. Every so often a rock splashed down near me, bringing with it laughter from shore. The rock throwing intervals increased and the rocks became larger. After two near misses, I paddled out further. The crew on shore stood up, moved closer to the water and threw sharp, dangerous rocks at us. Dave and I paddled north, toward the point.

The rocks continued to whiz by and the words screamed out by Big Sam pierced the already miserable day. "Don't come in until you catch a wave," he shouted.

I looked at Dave, and started to paddle for a small wave. "They mean the point," he screamed to me with fear in his voice as I pulled back without dropping into the little wave. We paddled north until we were in the channel just south of the point. Here we sat in deep water feeling the swells rise beneath us as we looked to see the waves unload less than 50 feet away. The swell continued to pump, and we shivered with cold and fear as the threats and rocks continued from shore.

I figured that we would either have to face the pain and humiliation by going to shore, or wait until they got tired of hassling us. I turned to explain my feeble plans to Dave, but I could see that something in him had changed. He no longer looked timidly in, but was focused fiercely, instead, on the rugged lines pouring into the point. Without saying a word he put his head down, and paddled away from me into the lineup where he was dwarfed by the first wave of the set. He wasn't planning on taking off, was he? Another smaller wave approached, and Dave paddled for it from the shoulder. He caught the wave and stood up while it was still double-overhead to him. I would have called that wave 12 foot at the time, now, maybe six. Still, it was far bigger than anything either of us had surfed before.

I was stroking toward Dave as he flew past me, nearly loosing the wave because he was so far out in front of the curl. Nervously, I kept an eye on him and on the horizon in case a set wave swung wide and nailed me. I was alone now, in a do-or-die situation, and no longer aware of the screams of our assailants. I concentrated only on catching the next wave, and tried to calm myself while my courage rose and fell and my blood pumped hard.

Without looking up, I paddled from the channel into the lineup, and stroked into position. Then I moved in on the biggest, darkest wave I had ever tried to catch.

I slid for a long time, bouncing into the trough where I did a slow bottom turn and sank down into a survival stance against the wall.

Then I hit chop and flew into a wipeout, which sent me down, and my board rolling toward shore and then over, into the channel. After breaking the surface I saw the board nearby. I swam in to retrieve it. The wave didn't hit me too hard, however, and the entire incident was over in seconds. But I no longer felt any fear for the waves, or, oddly, the boys on the beach. I paddled back out and caught the next wave, taking off at an angle, fighting the wind and chop, hanging on without turning. After a short ride, the wave released me in the channel in front of Dave who sat there hooting with his arms in the air.

Dave quieted down, but there remained a lot of shouting. We looked to the beach, where Dog, Stinky, Birdie, Frenchfry, and Big Sam lifted their arms and jumped on the rocks in celebration of our surfing, somehow feeling entitled to rob us of a part of our victory by making it theirs also.

For that one moment everything was perfect. I saw my younger brother as a hero, and we splashed each other, and laughed in the water like children, both with the unspoken knowledge that we had become real surfers.

"Forget those dopes, let's get another one," he said to me as we paddled back out and then surfed for about half an hour. On shore we were offered sugar doughnuts, licorice laces, and Red Mountain by the boys. We declined the wine, but ate until we were stuffed.

On the way home, Big Sam stopped at Safeway again. He made Birdie get out and leach money while Dave and I sat comfortably in the front seat of the car. Minutes later Birdie returned with his head low and a meager 85 cents in his hand. "Get in the back," Dave yelled at Birdie with his newly found authority. Big Sam smiled at Dave, turned a mean look on Birdie, ripped the money from his hand, and then pocketed it. As Birdie scampered back into the car Sam smiled and asked Dave "What should we do with that little bird; should we pants him?" Dave laughed hard and looked at Birdie who sat shriveled with his head down, behind us. We both knew that Big Sam would have no problem leaving Birdie tied naked to a telephone pole. It all depended on Dave now. Dave held Birdie's entire future in his hands but had enough compassion to let him off the hook.

As we drove home, Big Sam wrapped me in a warm towel and gave Dave his surf-club sweat shirt that Sam had given him to wear.

We never did tell Mom what had happened, but we were scolded by her for coming home without our church clothes on, covered instead by salt-crusted trunks, a towel, and a raggedy sweat shirt.

Mom got over it in a few days. And Big Sam? He turned out to be a pretty cool guy after all. In fact, he never did ask for his towel or his sweat shirt back.

*

# GARBAGE, LAWN RAKES, AND BUTTER-FLIES

## I

Three of us pulled up to the break called Garbage at Sunset Cliffs. There we stood on the bluff with a handful of surfers who, like us, were checking out the new north swell. The surf was three to five feet, slightly offshore, and moderately crowded. To the south, six or seven breaks peaked and folded one after another. To the north, a half dozen more breaks packed in 12 to 15 surfers each.

Nobody spoke as we scanned the area from Newbreak to Luscomb's, where a wave peeled about half a mile away from where we stood. One paddler looked familiar even from here—blond, tanned, knee paddling, stroking deeply and powerfully. It was obvious that he was riding a very long board.

Most of us had identified him even before he took a wave, and those standing near were also looking out to see the wave the rider would catch.

Spin around, no paddle, up, clean entry behind the peak, push the big board into a perfect turn. And then walk, glide like a pelican to the tip and back, into the cutback, and another turn, walk to the nose, not all the way to the tip, but about a foot from it—standing there parallel and arching with the wave breaking all around. Who would be the first to state the obvious. The signature kick out, never faltering, or breaking style sealed it.

As the man went from his feet to his knees, he did not touch the deck of the board with his hands. Now, all eyes were on him. He paddled back out without a decrease in his stride, a man at the height of his power at an age when most had retired to country-club sports.

As he paddled, two voices simultaneously blurted out what everyone knew. "That's Skip Frye," said the voices. The others nodded and smiled, and knew that they had witnessed a subtle but great athletic achievement, a minimalists" statement supreme.

## II

We were at San Onofre on a recent summer afternoon, parked next to Skip and Donna Frye's Dodge station wagon when Hank Warner walked up, and gave me the latest installment of his "life of a gremmie in San Diego." As usual, I was informed and entertained. Then Warner directed my attention to the top of Frye's car where a shovel and two rakes, "Frye's kit," he called it, lay stacked next to several very long boards. The shortest of the boards was owned and shaped by Mike Hynson, who was also along for the ride that day.

Frye, according to Warner, had come to the beach early, raked clean the petty discards of our plastic-driven society, and set up camp for himself and his friends in the clean sand. This he had done in the same style that he did everything, with care and eloquence. That was how he had built the steps at Pacific Beach Point for the elderly who for years had not been able to walk down the path and enjoy the edge of the sea.

Hank headed for the surf as Donna walked up, and, in her typically generous way offered food and sodas. She, like Hank, had a story about the man she loves.

"I have to tell you this," she said, trying unsuccessfully to withhold emotion. "The other day," she began, "the wind was blowing offshore, and Skip was out surfing in front of the shop at Crystal Pier. He had only ridden a few waves when he noticed a butterfly in the water. It had been blown out to sea, and was unable to get back to shore. Skip reached down, scooped up the butterfly, placed it in his still dry hair, and caught a wave, surfing it to the sand. Then he walked back to the shop, took the butterfly from his hair, and placed it on an Easter Lily that was resting on the counter."

Thinking that was the end of the story, I said, "Knowing Skip, he must have found some spiritual significance to that."

"Oh, yes, there was," replied Donna, who had not yet completed the tale. "My grandmother would jokingly ask Skip to take her surfing. Skip would always answer the same way, saying, 'I'll ride one for you today grandma.'"

"Right at the time my grandmother passed away, Skip was riding that wave with the butterfly."

A week or so after hearing the story, I strolled into Frye's shop, "Harry's," and walked up to the Easter Lily on the counter where the butterfly was perched, still attached to the heart of the flower. It had apparently passed from this harsh world as quietly as it had entered, and its wings were folded as if in silent prayer.

As I contemplated the significance of the story, Hank Warner, who shares the building with the Fryes, walked into the showroom, and over to the Easter Lily.

"At first I felt sorry for the little guy," said

Hank, referring to the butterfly. But then I thought, "Hey, how many butterflies have ever ridden a wave with Skip Frye?"

*Skip and Donna Frye live in Pacific Beach where they own Harry's Surf Shop along with Hank Warner. Frye builds some very long and beautiful surfboards.*

# GREG'S PAPERWEIGHT

Rick James is a free man. He works, pays taxes, and surfs whenever he wants to. But, while nobody owns the majority of his body, it is unclear who has the legal right to one of his thumbs. As you may know, Greg Noll took possession of the appendage 20-some years ago when James lost it in Noll's surf shop while cutting center strips on surfboard blanks with a power saw.

After Greg took Rick to the hospital, Greg wrapped up the bloody thumb and cast it in clear resin for safe keeping. He kept it in his surf shop showcase where shoppers stood in stunned disbelief to find a thumb amid the fins and sunglasses. Rick came in one day and asked Greg not to put his thumb on public display anymore. Greg obliged and, it is said, used the thumb as a paperweight in his office for many years.

After Noll closed his Hermosa Beach surf shop and moved to Northern California, he kept the thumb in storage along with other more common memorabilia. That was okay for the time, but now, in these days of $5,000-plus collectable surfboards, a well preserved body part of a notable shaper should fetch a fortune. Not that anyone's bidding on it, but if they did, who would own it?

Let's see, the thumb originally belonged to Rick James; Greg Noll rescued it before a nurse could dispose of it, and he (Noll) has had possession of it ever since. Greg may have had the thumb for longer than Rick did, but Rick grew it, kept the nail clipped and clean during its formative years, and used it for many practical tasks.

So, who owns the thumb?

Don't ask me. Still, given the trend in court cases, no reasonable judge would deny James anything less than joint custody.

Anyway, Rick, if you really want to see your thumb (his thumb?) again, I am told that Greg Noll keeps it on his nightstand and puts it to good use as a paperweight.

✳

*Greg Noll lives in Crescent City, California with his wife, Laura. He is involved with a clothing line, "Da Bull," builds wooden surfboards, fishes for salmon, and does whatever he wants.*

# THE SIMMONS LIBERATION ARMY

By Mace

*Until his death near Windansea Beach in 1953, Bob Simmons was one of the most influential surfboard designers of all times. As the following story proves, his boards have continued to inspire many young surfers in more ways than one.*

December 1991

You have a bourbon and water in the upstairs cocktail lounge of the La Jolla Cove Chart House. A relic of surf history lies shackled to the wall above you. Looking essentially like a tongue depressor with a rounded nose and a soft, wide squaretail, you realize that this board, for its time, was a very advanced piece of equipment.

The board's positioning in the room is rife with irony. It has a clear view through the tinted glass. Cold winter lines pour into the cove below, and the concussion of their slamming into the cliffs rattles the brass vines that secure the board to the wall. Constant marination in cigarette smoke has yellowed the board. Bits of petrified mud pie cling to its nose. A course Arizona tourist raps the board with his knuckles, perhaps wondering if it is hollow. But this board is anything but hollow. It was shaped by Bob Simmons with a drawknife and a hand planer. Instead of simply planing mild rocker in the nose, Simmons has glued an additional piece of balsa to the deck, and spooned out the package. A four inch deep radius fin was sunk into the tail.

You rattle your ice and begin to contemplate the shame the Simmons must feel. Twenty-nine years without a surf, no doubt feeling the ocean's pulse as it pounds the cliffs below. But hang on a second here...something's a bit askew. You stand up for closer inspection, and confirm your first glance. The board has been waxed.

September 1985

A wicked harvest moon was hanging high above the cliffs of Blacks Beach. The dark water of the cove shimmered and danced as it reflected off the sandstone. High above, the lights of the restaurant were clicking off: one...two...and now all was dark. Three men clad only in surf trunks darted up the stairs. They quietly stared 20 feet above them, to the open window. Stealthily, they rolled a dumpster against the wall and crawled onto its lid. Forming a human pyramid, they came within inches of the ledge. Kurt, the most nimble of the three, made a game leap and pulled himself through. From inside, the sound of rattling metal. The two left outside envisioned Kurt pulling apart the brass vines. A shape took form as it emerged through the window. The Simmons felt fresh air for the first time in decades. Gingerly, the heavy board was lowered to the ground. Checking for bystanders, the group ran the board across Cave Street and opened a hidden gate in the shell shop fence.

Cloistered behind the fence and hidden from view, the ceremony began. Murmured chants, quiet chuckling and the clinking of glasses. A splash of red wine was poured down the length of the Simmons, now sporting a fresh layer of wax.

This event had been planned for six months. Tide books and wave journals had been consulted. This night had been chosen over all others for numerous reasons: full moon, probability of swell and slim prospects of police interference. The preparations had, thus far, paid off. The ceremony wailed on to a crescendo.

Hoots and howls pierced the silence. The board was loaded into a truck and driven to the reef at North Bird. The three men stared through the windshield at the little moonlit bay. Solid eight-footers reared up out of the kelp and threw themselves into the shallows. The rumble of the whitewater was accentuated by the quiet of the streets. Kurt, a veteran of North Bird and a rider of archaic surf vehicles, was elected to complete the ritual. Knee-paddling through the calm channel, the board seemed to come alive. Every stroke yielded a ten yard glide, and even with its nub of a fin the board tracked a true line. Almost immediately, a set lifted out of the darkness and Kurt stroked into a bloated, chocolate chip shaped peak. The wave went past vertical and Kurt, totally committed, pearled up to his throat. The Simmons blew out of the whitewater and glided into the channel, glistening. He swam over, retrieved it, and paddled back out. The next wave hit the reef at exactly the right angle. The face went concave as the wave dragged the bottom, and Kurt was already up and hissing left. After the initial top turn, the board accelerated dramatically. A little check turn put him back up high, then he leaned into a long, arcing cutback towards the soup. His cronies on the cliff went wild.

After three more waves, the board was secured under a pile of kelp in a small, wind carved grotto. The crew drove back to the shell shop to devise a means to return the board. It was now dawn. As they rounded the corner, their jaws dropped. A police car was in their parking space and the Chart House manager and two Jack Webb types were on the balcony. The crew continued driving, unseen.

September 1953

Bob Simmons and Dempsy Holder are sanding out the last bumps on the latest craft. Simmons has mixed emotions. He knows that this board is a full 40 pounds lighter than any predecessors. He also knows that this could lead to something as yet unseen in California: the appearance of crowds. For now he's stoked. The board has a flexible, resilient quality about it. He pictures it performing well on steep, deep-water waves like the Tijuana Sloughs, Windansea and North Bird. He and Dempsy load it up and head to the beach. Simmons paddles it out to the second peak, the Los Coronados crystal clear behind him. He lifts his gimp arm and waves to his buddy outside. It's eight feet and clean.

*

# GREENHORN IS COWBOY FOR KOOK

*The smoking revolver jumped in my left hand as I laughed wildly, and little brother lay beneath me, dead on the front lawn. Mother ran across the yard screaming hysterically. I was frozen with fear as I watched her charge over the damp grass waving her arms. Then I hung my head and cried as she pried my fingers loose from the pistol for the last time. "You're 14 years old," she yelled. "You're too old to play cowboys."*

By the summer of 1967 I was a surfer. But surfing was becoming repetitive and I wanted something more. I was 18 years old, and had dropped toy guns but not gun-slinging notions. Shoulder-length black hair and Indian beads hid the cowboy within. I lived with my parents and younger brother, Dave, in the house where we were raised, a hundred years and a thousand miles beyond cattle country, near East LA, just a few miles from Sunset Strip and Hollywood, California where I hung out weekend nights.

Eventually I hated Hollywood as much as I did the stupid revolution being waged at my doorstep. While most surfers became hippies and burned with Jimi Hendrix and Janice Joplin, my aching heart rode side-saddle with Hank Williams. I worshiped John Wayne and had seen every one of his movies. As a closet cowboy, I often slapped *Rodeo Magazine* between the pages of the *LA Free Press* — and it was *Rodeo Magazine* that changed my life.

Miraculously the advertisement jumped from one of its back pages: "Experienced Cowhands Wanted. Send Qualifications to: Donald Fredericks, Triple-D Ranch, Horse Mountain, Nevada."

I sent Fredericks a letter that day — told

him that my brother and I had grown up riding and breaking horses on our family's ranch. What a lie! We had rented a few broken-down mares at Griffith Park a few times, and while we had ridden well, we were not good enough to justify the fantasy of being real cowboys.

All that next week I rifled through the mail until the day I found the letter sealed within the official Triple-D envelope. My hands shook as I read :

Dear Mister Ahrens:

Thank you for your kind letter. You and your brother can start work immediately. The pay, including room and board, is $180.00 a month.

Sincerely,

Donald Fredericks

Foreman, Triple-D Ranch

Horse Mountain, Nevada

I dropped the letter onto the floor and let out a loud whoop. I was on my way out to ride the range.

After lying about our wages, I convinced Dave to join me, telling him that it was a good way to earn enough money for Hawaii that coming winter. With the money received from selling our surfboards and the little we had saved, we bought cowboy hats, boots, and a couple tins of *Red Man Chewing Tobacco*. We quickly packed the car and said good-bye to friends and family who stood waving from our parent's driveway.

Free for the first time, I switched the car radio from rock to country, turned it up good and loud and packed my cheek with *Red Man*. Then I floored it for Tonopah, in my souped-up '55 Chevy that I hoped to trade in for a horse and a pickup truck.

In Tonopah, my car with its screaming

yellow flames, and California plates attracted a lot of attention, especially from a pack of young girls. An instant blonde, a not unpleasant looking hippie girl in hip-huggers and an Indian blouse, seemed particularly interested. She eyed the car, slinked over, and introduced herself as Phyllis. "You boys want to come to a party?" she asked.

"No thanks. We're on our way to the town of Horse Mountain." I said.

"It's no town, it's just a mountain," she said laughing. The other girls giggled lightly but kept their distance. Phyllis was doing the talking. "What are you doing here anyway? This place is dead," said Phyllis. Then she spat out her gum, lit up a cigarette, and blew the smoke into the bright blue air.

"We're on our way to the Triple-D Ranch; you know where it is?"

"The 3-D? Yeah, I know. Just follow 8-A west, and look for the sign on the right hand side of the road."

"How far is it?"

"'Bout 80 miles."

"What's the next town?"

"No town between here and Horse Mountain, just tumble weeds and cow crap," she said while turning her gaze away from me to Dave. Then, in a convincing display of hurt feelings she said, "You sure you don't want to come to my party?"

"Maybe we can party next weekend," replied Dave with a smile.

"Yeah, okay. I'll see you next weekend," she said in a sexy voice. She wrote her phone number on the back of a matchbook and threw it into Dave's lap.

It was nearly midnight when we roared

into the 3-D, which is what we were calling it now. A towering, square-framed man with a 55-gallon-drum of a hat practiced lassoing fence posts beneath a naked light bulb in an otherwise empty corral. As we broke dust and silence, he faced us and watched as the loud Chevy approached. He stood straight and silent with one hand on his hip, as if we were in a showdown together. He didn't move as I parked and began walking toward him, talking fast and extending my hand while still a horse's tail away. "Hi, you the foreman? You Mister Fredericks?" I asked.

"Nope," he replied slowly, before spitting in the dust, straightening his big hat and looking down at me. "I'm just one of the buckaroos." My hand still extended, I nearly swallowed the chaw in my mouth, but somehow kept from laughing. Dave, who always laughs at the wrong times, doubled over and walked back to the car where he fell into a fit of laughter. We had only heard words like buckaroos spoken by Gabby Hayes in old movies. I struggled to keep control, but Dave's distant howls caused me to laugh right into the big man's face.

Without moving or saying a word the buckaroo wiped my spray from his face with his bandanna. "Sorry," I said. "We just heard a great joke and haven't gotten over it yet." He didn't change expression, but I'm sure he didn't buy my lame excuse. Again, I put my hand forward saying, "My name's Chris."

Crushing my hand, and looking me dead in the eye he said in a deep voice, "Name's Stumpy." Dave overheard the name and laughed again, louder this time. Still within Stumpy's grasp, I laughed hard in his face again. His eyes narrowed like Clint Eastwood just before someone made his day. He yanked his big hand away.

Wiping his face with his bandanna again, he growled, "follow me," and stomped away on the hard dirt.

I followed Stumpy on foot, threw the keys to Dave and told him to shut up and tail us in the car. I walked silently behind Stumpy to the bunkhouse, a stark, rectangular wooden box filled with the sounds of loudly snoring men. Stumpy said nothing as we entered, just threw us a couple of blankets and left. We bedded down in a corner, as far from the others as possible. It was dark and cold when I was awoken by something sharp poking me the ribs, and a deep voice saying, "Get up, get dressed and follow me." It was Stumpy.

Dave took a swing at me when I shook him awake but I yanked him out of his bunk, still dressed in his clothes from the night before. He just shuffled along tiredly behind us as I tried making friendly conversation with Stumpy, who walked a few paces ahead of me. Stumpy didn't react to anything I said, he just walked and looked at the ground. When he finally did speak, his words weren't directed at me or anyone else. "Fredericks is the owner of the Triple-D," he said, "but he ain't no cattleman—never has been. The idiot's a banker from Hollywood that thinks it's fun raisin' beef. Hell, he don't raise the beef, I do." He spat a load of brown tobacco juice on the ground to punctuate the statement.

Parked next to a bronzed horse hitch was a big, four-wheel drive truck with cowhide seat covers and the flaming Triple-D brand delicately painted onto both doors along with cowboys chasing ethereal cattle through the clouds. We walked the clean oak stairs to the leaded glass and oak door that guarded the entry of a two-story, luxury bunkhouse. Stumpy knocked. Moments later the man I would come to know as Donald Fredericks answered.

Fredericks looked too frail for the wild west, more like Don Knotts than John Wayne. He was a withered man—about five-four, 120 pounds with thinning gray hair and a mousy, gray moustache. He led the fashion roundup in designer jeans, a silky black cowboy shirt, matching bandanna, gray lizard boots, and a small, delicate off-white cowboy hat that he wore tilted slightly to one side. Chopin mixed awkwardly with moose and buffalo heads, western art, and Greek sculpture.

Fredericks smiled like Cal Worthington winding up to sell the entire herd of Dodge vans. "Welcome gents, you must be the Ahrens brothers," he said, holding out his dainty, white hand.

"Yes sir," I replied enthusiastically. "I'm Chris Ahrens and this is my brother, Dave." Dave barely lifted his tired hand to shake.

Fredericks asked us to be seated. He motioned for us to sit on the deerskin-covered couch. "Coffee or herb tea, gents?" he asked, holding up two steaming teapots both bearing the Triple-D brand. Stumpy rolled his eyes and ordered black coffee. The rest of us drank tea.

Fredericks explained that he had built the place up from nothing to one of the biggest herds in Nevada while Stumpy wrung his hands together tightly as he looked to the floor. After a brief history of his life, Fredericks smiled, winked, and patted my leg. "You won't need to break horses for a while," he said as I pulled my leg away hoping that he would move away from me and that Dave wouldn't laugh. I was relieved that neither of them reacted in the way I feared. Fredericks continued, "You'll mend fences and go on an occasional cattle drive. Stumpy here will be your boss, and he'll cut out horses for you when you need 'em."

"Thank you, Mister Fredericks," I said calmly as I shook his soft hand before leaving the house.

After a breakfast of ham and eggs at headquarters, Stumpy walked us over to a corral full of fat, lazy cows and said "I don't care what that little chipmunk told you, no greenhorns are ever ridin' my horses." Stumpy smiled, looked straight at me, and with a slight laugh said, "You boys are gonna' herd cattle all right—on foot!"

Stumpy introduced us to Hank, our supervisor, and walked away to saddle up. Moments later he rode past us with the other cowboys as they laughed and hollered, and rode into the sunrise. Hank shrugged his shoulders in resignation of our horseless fate, but his partner, Dennis, gave an admiring look at the cowboys as they passed. "Sure do wish I could ride with 'em," said Dennis as he watched them ride off.

Hank was a short, nervous, nail biter of about 30 with spiky brown hair expanding from a three week old crewcut. He had been fired from "Green Giant" in Idaho for rustling vegetables, and had answered the same advertisement as we had in *Rodeo*. On his way to the ranch he met Dennis, a tall, flabby-hearted bookkeeper from Chicago.

Dennis kept asking us for pictures and phone numbers of girls that we knew. Worn out by his repeated pleading, I produced a wallet photo of Poly, my girlfriend from home. Her phone number was written over the photo. Dennis looked at the shot and handed it back without comment. I figured that he didn't like her looks much.

Later that day he told me that Poly was a

bitch. I was amazed by how much he had learned from just one photo, and admired his gift of discernment. Only when I returned to Hollywood did I discover that Dennis had memorized her number, called her, and proposed marriage. Thinking that it was me disguising my voice, Poly said yes to the proposal, and went along with the joke for a while. When she realized that it was a stranger on the phone, and that he was serious, she slammed down the receiver. Dennis had called back five or six times, and each time Poly hung up on him.

Dennis broke into tears as he told me about another heartbreak. He was on his way to Los Angeles from Chicago to marry a girl whom he had spoken to only once over the phone. His car broke down in Tonopah. That's where he met Hank, heard about the 3-D, and hitchhiked to the ranch.

Hank didn't care for ranch life, but Dennis loved it. In fact he loved it so much that he had left his long-distance bride at the altar. He didn't contact her until two weeks after the wedding date. Then he called to ask if she wanted to be a cowboy's wife. He claimed that he was a ruined man ever since she changed phone numbers.

Dennis was also a storehouse of hopefully inaccurate information on everybody at the ranch. After cluing us in on the weirdness of some of the hands, he asked, "you guys met Sam yet?"

"No," I replied.

"Well, stay away from him. He shot and killed a man and buried him on the range. He hates you hippie types, and he's real mean. Once he tried to get me to herd a corral full of bulls. He told me they were cows, and nearly got me trampled to death." Dave and I laughed loudly, but I was nervous about meeting Sam.

After shoving cows around until dark, Hank and Dennis showed us to the TV room where Dave and I sunk into an old sofa. Hank's eyes grew wide as we sat down. "Don't sit there," he said, "that's for buckaroos only." Hank and Dennis didn't see anything funny, but we were laughing so hard that they began laughing also.

As we sat laughing, Stumpy and the man named Sam led the other hands into the room. They seemed startled by our trespasses. Dave continued laughing, stood up, and held out his hands to shake with Sam, who slapped it away. Then we simultaneously noticed Sam's six-gun, a dark piece of metal protruding from a worn leather holster. I began to think that Dennis might have been telling the truth about Sam murdering a man. Quietly defeated, Dave and I returned to the wooden benches where we sat with the other greenhorns. The cowboys made under-the-breath remarks about us as we walked back to our seats.

Dave and I took our abuse silently, but Dennis boldly asked to borrow a smoke from Sam, of all people. Sam shook the pack and a couple of cigarettes popped out of the top. He held them out to Dennis who started over to get one when he was tripped by one of the boys. Everybody laughed except Dave, Hank, and I. Even Dennis laughed a little, in a slightly humiliated way that he was familiar with. But he dusted himself off and continued walking to get his smoke.

Sam grinned at me through his broken yellow and gold teeth, silently daring me to say something. Dennis' warning about Sam kept me quiet. I looked away as Sam laughed meanly.

Dennis was tripped again on his return to the bench, but he held the cigarette up like a trophy, proud that he hadn't broken it. Then he sat down, lit up and watched "*The Monkees*", with the rest of the cowboys.

Sam whispered something to Stumpy. The two men laughed as Sam nodded and then asked Dennis, "Hey partner, how'd you like to join us in the branding tomorrow?"

"Me? Sure would," replied Dennis brightly.

"Okay be ready to ride at dawn," said Sam. Without another word Dennis ran from the room.

I didn't see him again until late that night when he woke me by turning on the light over my bunk. "Well, how do I look?" he asked. To be truthful, he looked really dumb in the shiny black hat, cheap naugahyde chaps and tinny spurs attached to his patent-leather black boots. He looked like Captain Kangaroo dressed up to play Jesse James. He looked like Dennis the bookkeeper going out to trick-or-treat. But he stood proudly at the foot of my bed, drew a pretend six-shooter with his finger and said, "draw partner."

"You look great Dennis," I said shielding my face from the light. "Now turn off the light and go to sleep."

He shot his finger at me again, and said, "Yeah, I do look pretty good, don't I." He finally turned out the light, but woke me nearly every hour when he switched it on again to check the time and spit on his new boots.

That morning after breakfast, Dave and I dragged over to mend fences while Dennis bounced along ready to saddle up and ride. I was jealous at first, but after a few hard falls trying to put on the saddle and mount his horse, I felt sorry for him. When he finally did get the saddle on, he looked our way, waved his hat and yelled,

"Giddyup!" The horse stood still. Kicking and swearing, Dennis had no luck until suddenly the animal took off and burst past us and the other cowboys. He rode deep into the prairie, somehow hanging on while the men shouted mock encouragement at him.

By mid-day, roughly 100 calves had been rounded up and brought back to the corral near our working area. Dennis rode in a full half-an-hour behind the others. His clothes were torn and filthy, his chaps were scuffed, and he had a big bump on his forehead. But he smiled, sat straight in the saddle and gave us "thumbs up" as he rode past.

Being kind of proud of Dennis I returned the gesture, but the cowboys made crude fun of him. These men were nothing like the ones I had seen in *The War Wagon* or *High Noon*. They were small, petty men, not worthy of shinning "Shane's" belt buckle.

Still, there was something great about them when they rode from the saddle. I watched Stumpy turn his cutting horse perfectly into the herd, pick out a calf, work it to the edge, toss his rope around his hind legs and pull it to the flankers for branding. He rode tall and was quick, powerful and commanding, with a delicate touch when necessary. For that one moment he was my hero. But he was transformed quickly as he climbed down from his horse, looked at me and said, "What are you lookin' at, Greenhorn?"

We had been at the 3-D for three weeks, and Dave and I were still herding cattle on foot. We worked hard from sunup to sundown, six and a half days a week. One day after work I was so tired that I fell asleep on the couch. I awoke suddenly with something poking me in the ribs.

I pushed the blunt object away, and then opened my eyes to see that it was Sam prodding me with his pistol. "Move or die," he growled. I sat up too tired to react at first. "Move or die," he repeated. I moved.

The other cowboys made their usual mean remarks as they passed. Dennis, who now rode with them regularly, brought up the rear. He stomped past us without looking our way. His thumbs were tucked beneath his belt as he marched over to the couch and sat down between Sam and Stumpy like they were all old friends.

"Hey Dennis, how'd you do today?" asked Hank sincerely. Dennis struck a match on the sole of his boot, lit a Marlboro, took a deep drag, exhaled and looked coldly at the three of us.

"You greenhorns probably think it's a lot of fun ridin' the range, don't you?" snapped Dennis. Even Dave was too shocked to laugh. We had lost Dennis.

Two days later, Dave led Hank and I to the bunkhouse refrigerator just before chow time. He pulled out a long, plump rainbow trout and held it by the gillplate with his index finger. Then he told us about a little pond nearby that was packed with fish. He had made a hook from a straight pin, tied a piece of cotton string to it, baited it with roast beef, and pulled in the fish in less than a minute. We fried up the trout on the hotplate with some potatoes that Hank had rustled from headquarters. After dinner, we threw the remains of our feast into the trash.

It was dark when we walked to the pond. There we saw Sam with a big net, hauling in fish and putting them into a sack. We watched him from a safe distance as he filled several sacks, put them into his truck, and drove off, probably to sell them in town. It seemed that Sam had taken all the fish, because we didn't catch anything that night.

It was a few days before Hank told us that

Fredericks was mad as hell, and had ordered a meeting of all hands after morning chow. "If Fredericks is mad it must be serious," I said.

"Yeah, the cleaners must have gone on strike," said Dave, making fun of the cowboys' immaculate, little outfits. Dave and Hank laughed, but I figured that we were in for some trouble.

Donald Fredericks sat, resplendent in his matching red Sunday outfit, at the head of the table, and tried to make his voice sound bigger than the mousy squeak it always was.

"Men," he said "it has come to my attention that somebody's been fishin'." Raising his voice, he looked directly at me and continued. "My private breeding pond, the one I use to stock the local rivers with has been completely fished out!"

He pounded the table, barely restraining his tiny fist from landing too hard on the wood. Fredericks took a deep breath and paused to calm himself. He was hyperventilating. Fred, the cook, slapped him on the back. Nobody else dared to speak, but the boys threw occasional fierce glances at me and Dave. They figured that we'd done it for sure. Luckily Dave looked away from the comical sight of Fredericks' red face, or he could not have controlled the need to laugh, and the cowboys might have finished us off right there.

Fredericks drew a deep breath, calmed down a little and continued his speech. "Now, I'm not going to accuse anybody, he said, but I expect the guilty party to come forward and see me privately. I will not press charges, but I will dock the man's pay accordingly. I think that's more than fair."

Fredericks said that he would be eating at headquarters the next morning and would announce "future drastic measures if the guilty party didn't fess up." He looked at me much of the time as he spoke, with an expression moms use when they're "disappointed, not angry." Most of the other cowboys were looking at me too. They were angry.

Quietly, we walked out the back door to avoid confrontation. Being Sunday, we only worked half day. We skipped lunch and drove to the local bar a few miles up the road where we played pool, had a few beers and discussed our strategy. Nobody would believe that Sam had done it. Even if they did, it would be suicide to tell Fredericks. So, with no other options, we decided to sneak out in the morning. Fredericks could keep the pay he owed us.

Even though he'd been such a jerk to us, we decided to see Dennis again. He was shining his boots on his bunk, and when he saw us approaching, he flinched and looked back to his work. We didn't tell him that we were leaving, but Dave stuck out his hand and shook with him, saying that we wanted to be friends again. To assure good intentions, Dave handed Dennis the matchbook with Phyllis' number on it, the girl we had met in Tonopah nearly a month earlier. Dennis looked at the phone number, smiled broadly, thanked Dave and shook hands with each of us.

That night Dave and I found rotten fish heads under our pillows—something we interpreted as a cowboy's cheap "Godfather" trick. After a light sleep, we woke an hour earlier than usual, packed the car and filled the tank from Fredericks' private gas pump. He owed us at least that much.

Hiding in the bushes surrounding the bunkhouse, we caught stray phrases about "getting rid of hippies." Dave gagged himself with his own hand to keep from laughing. When the cowboys were beyond sight we both laughed hard. We returned inside, and put the fish heads into Sam's pillow, and Dave scratched "sucks" beneath the hat peg bearing Sam's name. Laughing with joyful destruction, we filled Sam's extra pair of boots with fish guts.

Then we peeled out for headquarters where I spun doughnuts in the dust, and blasted my horn. Fredericks and Sam led a furious pack of cowboys who foolishly charged the car. Hank stood behind them looking shocked and confused. In his frenzy, Fredericks ran toward the car and slung a small rock from his shoulder, in the way you would throw a shot-put. The rock bounced lightly off of the window, and we laughed until I remembered that Sam was armed. When I mentioned the fact to Dave, it made him laugh even harder. I slammed the throttle to the floor and sprayed Fredericks with his own dirt and gravel. When the dust cleared, we could see him raising his little fists, screaming and jumping up and down. The white outfit was filthy.

My wheels sunk into the dust a little as we skidded and swerved and headed for the main gate hoping that it would be open. Stumpy, Sam, and Fredericks piled into the 3-D truck which was parked in front of headquarters. Stumpy drove. The gate was open, and we pulled onto the main highway with Fredericks' truck close behind.

The other cowboys split up into two old company trucks, but they were so slow that we never saw them again. Fredericks' truck was pretty fast, however, and I let him get close enough to think he had us. From my rear-view mirror I watched them gain on us. I laughed to see Fredericks jerk around in his seat like a furious squirrel. Dave, who had not quit laughing since we hit the road, turned around and exploded with laughter when he saw Fredericks. I looked back again to see that Sam wore a dangerous look, like he was ready to kill us. Stumpy wore a satisfied half-smile, like he was glad to see Fredericks get worked over by somebody.

Sam raised his gun toward my car as adrenaline shot through me and I floored it instinctively. No shot was ever fired, however. Stumpy, who slowed the company truck to a near stop, must have restrained Sam from shooting at us.

I floored it and felt the power of my 409 kick in as I looked in my rear-view mirror to see the 3-D truck and ranch fade from view forever. I kept moving fast, knowing that Sam and Fredericks would be after us as soon as they saw our handiwork in the bunkhouse.

We didn't slow down until we hit Tonopah, where, for the first time, I wondered; where had Dennis been the entire time? Cruising down the main street, I caught sight of a man dressed in white bell-bottoms, a paisley shirt and a beaded Indian headband. Dennis! He looked like a store-bought hippie. We couldn't stop to talk, but honked and waved. He flashed us the peace sign with one hand. With the other hand he held onto Phyllis.

★

# BURNT OFFERINGS

In the early '50s Malibu was the prime destination of all California surfers. Lured by perfect waves and a simple life, many slept on the sand, hoping to be the first ones out on a south swell. Bobby "Flea" Patterson, Charley Riemers, and Mickey Muñoz were among the kids who camped there regularly.

One night they sat around the fire drinking cheap wine and talking story. As the wine kicked in, Charley was first to fall into a deep sleep. As he snored in his sleeping bag, Bobby took a long pull from the jug and came up with an idea. "Let's burn Charley's board," he said.

"Come on Flea, we can't do that," replied Mickey.

"Yeah, let's burn it. He always over charges us for gas money, and, and ... Let's just burn it," said Bobby laughing as he pulled the board from the sand and Mickey half willingly helped him to shove it into the fire. The board began to smoke and Muñoz yelled, "Okay, that's enough, that's enough. It's burning. It's really burning."

"It's okay. It's okay. Leave it in. Leave it in," replied Flea as he blocked Mickey's attempts to retrieve the board, and laughed in perverse satisfaction, as the smoke began to billow. The board cooked for a while, when suddenly the hard-heated Flea repented of the act and pulled the balsa from the flames. The fire had left a wide circle of ugly black charcoal in the center of the beautiful white wood. Mickey helped Flea throw sand on the board in order to quench the fire. They left some sand on the deck in a vain attempt to hide the burn marks. The scars on the board's face were deep, however, and they refused cosmetic masking. After putting the fire completely out, Bobby and Mickey rolled into their sleeping bags and fell into a deep sleep until morning.

Muñoz awoke to see Patterson come to life, brush his tangled hair with his fingers and shake the sand and his hangover off as best he could.

The winds were warm and offshore, and they knew that they were in for another perfect day of three to five foot surf.

Then came remembrance and remorse as the details of last night's sacrifice began to creep back upon them. Fearfully, Mickey turned to wake Charley. He wasn't there. Mickey and the Flea looked out to sea, and there was Charley catching a beautiful wave and trimming up high to make his way into the cove.

Bobby looked around in confusion as Mickey grabbed his own board, shrugged to the Flea and ran for the water. Then, digging frantically in the sand, Flea saw something familiar, familiar except for the hole burned into the deck. Bobby Patterson had burned his own board.

*

# ALLOW ME TO INTRODUCE MY FRIEND

I first met Margo Godrey (now Margo Oberg) in the summer of 1970 when she was living in a friend's front yard in Cardiff, California in a pup tent. Margo was 16, recently transplanted from Santa Barbara, and filled with surf stoke and adventure.

We became friends and took short trips to northern Baja and Trestles together where she surfed brilliantly, and play a very bad harmonica. Other than that she was a good travel companion. We hung out a lot, but I usually went to Trestles alone. Before phone-in surf reports it was a great way to escape North County's crowds and summer flatness. During one decent-sized south swell I walked into Cotton's Point, the left at the northern tip of Trestles. The sets were in the six to eight foot range and Corky Carroll was out getting the best waves in each set. I paddled out too but was soon frustrated by Corky's aggression, and paddled behind him. He was throwing the first twin-fin I had ever seen up into new places on the wave. The board couldn't have been any longer than 5'10". It was an interesting design to me but I was a die-hard proponent of Brewer diamond tails, and even though our abilities were miles apart, I believed that my board would help me to edge out Corky in the speed department. I took off behind him on several waves. It was his spot, so I didn't feel bad about surfing behind him until I lost my board and had to swim to the beach to recover it.

I did not know it then, but I know now that Corky did not see my board because of his vision problems. He passed the board and paddled back into the break. I swore at him as he went by, and he glared at me in disbelief. I said some other stupid things and he stopped to find out what my problem was. This was the first time I had spoken to Carroll and I was screaming like an idiot. (This, I now realize, was a learned behavior from my youth. Nobody ever said so, but I knew that if you couldn't be a surf star, the next best thing was to hassle one. I would like to take this opportunity to apologize.) Anyway, Corky just said a few choice and sarcastic words to me, and I swam in, retrieved my board and paddled back out. Back in the lineup there were more waves and bad vibes. I rode a few more waves, walked back to my car and drove home.

The next evening Margo and I packed up my station wagon and headed for Santa Barbara, where we would stay at her mom's house and surf Jalama for a few days.

Knowing that Margo and Corky were friends, I said nothing about the incident with him as we cruised north, me turning up the radio to drown out her harmonica playing. When we got to San Clemente, Margo directed me to her friend's house. Thinking that she was trying to set me up with one of her girlfriends, I was glad to go wherever she wanted. I soon found myself at the door of an average-looking tract home. "Who lives here?" I asked her as she took the key from under the mat and opened the door.

"Just a friend, a really good friend," she said smiling broadly. With that she walked into the front room and then into the kitchen which was in the direct line of vision to the front door.

"These are really good friends of mine," she reassured me, noting my uncertainty as she opened the refrigerator door. I stood, half starving, next to a filled refrigerator, and she said, "Go ahead, make yourself something to eat." She giggled lightly and then excused herself as she walked to the bathroom. I had no intention of eating anything from the refrigerator, but I stood confused, in the kitchen with the refrigerator door opened.

Then I heard the front door creak open, and looked up in horror to see Margo's good friend, Corky Carroll. Corky Carroll! Margo was nowhere in sight and here I was, the idiot who had hassled him the day before. In his house! In his refrigerator! Apparently eating his food! At first he stood there in shocked surprise. Then he walked forward as if stalking me. Anger punctuated each of his steps. I could see what he was thinking, but I had no time to explain.

It was only seconds, very long seconds, before Margo walked into the front room and was greeted by Corky and his family. Corky registered surprise and confusion and Margo formally introduced me to him, his wife, Cheryl, and his son, Clint. I pretended to be meeting Corky for the first time. Whether he was merely being gracious, or he did not recognize me from the previous day, I do not know, but he showed no signs of recognition as we shook hands.

That evening we sat in the Carroll's front room and I listened to Corky and Margo talk about old friends they knew through surfing. He pulled out his guitar and began to play and sing. I had not yet regained my balance and was still too uncomfortable to speak. Just when I thought that things couldn't get any worse, Margo went for her harmonica.

✳

*Corky Carroll lives in Huntington Beach. He teaches tennis, writes magazine articles, acts in TV commercials, and surfs often. Margo Oberg lives with her family in Kauai.*

# MICKEY MAKES VARSITY

*On a December day in 1957 a small group of kids from California paddled out to Waimea Bay for the first time, and broke the size barrier. This was no easy task, especially in the pre-leash days of awkward boards. Without surf reports, nobody had a clue as to how big the swell might get. The memory of Dickie Cross, the surfer who died at Waimea while trying to paddle in from Sunset Beach, was still fresh in their minds. These were the facts. The rumors were even more frightening. Many said Waimea was a breeding ground for great white sharks. Others pointed out the ancient Hawaiian burial ground above the Waimea Valley and claimed that the bay was haunted. All of this swam in the head of a young teen-ager named Mickey Muñoz as he sat in the sand with a few friends and contemplated riding the biggest waves in the world.*

High school was a drag for an athletic kid who was too short for basketball, and too light for football. He was a surfer, something that nobody but the two other surfers at Santa Monica High understood. Because he had chosen this sport and was not built suitably for the others, he was made to feel a little inferior. Quarterbacks got the glory and the girl. Linebackers took what was left over. But there was something powerful boiling inside of Mickey Muñoz that none of his classmates knew about. He had drive, skill, and courage that were caged within the confines of the little school.

His classmates would never see it, but it didn't matter. One December day in 1957 Mickey's mom found this note on the kitchen table: "Dear mom, Going to Hawaii. Love, Mickey. P.S. I will write."

Hawaii was a surfers dream, and Mickey found that many people there valued surfing more than football. In the first week he had surfed Sunset, Pupukea, Makaha, all of the name spots. Now he faced 12 to 15 foot Waimea Bay. There were second thoughts. But there was also a good channel, and the waves, while big, were not much bigger than the ones he had ridden at Sunset a few days earlier. He figured that he could handle the drop, and really, that seemed to be the big challenge out there. No, the waves didn't really bother him that much. What really scared him were the sharks, or the stories of sharks—he had heard that the bay was swarming with great whites. Losing a board out there could be a fatal mistake.

But together with a crew which included Greg Noll, Harry Church, Pat Curren, Del Cannon, Bing Copeland and Mike Stange, Mickey paddled out, looking down occasionally in hopes that he would not see the white teeth of death. Church had caught a wave, maybe the first wave that day, and he was inside. That's when Muñoz decided to take off. He watched for the wave he wanted. It built far outside, flattened out, and then stood up on the reef where he spun around to meet it. He paddled hard down the face, but the 9'6" balsa board built for Malibu, had some severe design limitations. Bouncing to the bottom, he, nonetheless, stayed on his board, hanging on only because of his determination not to be eaten by a shark.

Having been schooled by Buzzy Trent to take off deep, Muñoz rode deeper than anyone else that day. Too deep. The wave exploded around him, and with no place to go, he

69

straightened out into a mass of soup. The surging water threatened to tear the board from his hands. But he could feel the sharks breathing, circling, waiting for blood, and so he hung on tightly. He lay there proned out, digging his fingers into the board, and then wrapping his arms and legs around the thing as he bounced toward shore. The rushing water impaired his vision, but as the soup subsided a bit, he was able to see a clear path to shore. He was going to make it in without having to swim.

Then, directly in front of him, he saw Church holding onto his board, preparing to duck through the wave. To continue the line would be to run him over. If he abandoned his board he would be shark food. Hitting Harry would not mean certain death, so Muñoz held on and somehow bounced over or around Church, narrowly missing him.

The crew surfed all morning, pushing each other into big waves. They did not return to shore until about 12:30 when one at a time they fell stoked and exhausted onto the sand. With no idea of making history, they sat on the beach and shared stories of their rides, most of which had resulted in wipeouts.

Finally the inner voice of Ricky Grigg, who used to say, "Take-off you chicken -shit little bastard," was beginning to subside inside of Mickey. He watched a huge set approach. Somebody took off, and the wave dwarfed him. "My God, look at the size of that wave!" said Muñoz. Then someone in the crowd answered, "You rode a lot of waves that size." Muñoz could not believe his accomplishment.

Eventually the clouds came and the small crowd left, leaving only Noll, Stange, and Muñoz to face the increasing swell. As they contemplated the surf, a disruptive bulldozer pulled up to the beach, and plowed open the mouth of the river. The water came rushing out, creating a massive rip, something which further compounded the seriousness of the situation.

Evening was approaching, and it was drizzling lightly when Muñoz and Stange, the two smallest surfers on the North Shore paddled out again. Noll stayed on the beach with his movie camera. The waves continued to build and they rode them bravely and alone. There they were, two wild kids on a break from high school, out in 20 foot-plus surf. The rain came and the wind howled as tension built. Stange, who had been in a high school drama class, sat up on his board and recited lines from Shakespeare. From far across the bay, Muñoz countered with lines of his own. Through the wind and rain Stange turned to Muñoz, and said in a loud voice, slightly muffled by the sounds of wind and breaking waves, "I took the uncircumcised dog by the throat, and smote him to death like this." With that he thrust an imaginary dagger into his chest, and rolled off his board into the water, remounting just in time to see massive lines on the horizon.

As they paddled out, they screamed back and forth to each other until they were electric with adrenaline. A set marched in bigger than any they had seen so far. It feathered in the middle of the bay and threatened to close out. Again Mickey contemplated the haunting words of Grigg "Take off you chicken- shit little bastard. Take off."

By now Mickey was weary of the constant pounding he had taken from riding deeper than anyone else that day. He yelled to Mike from the shoulder, "I'm not going over any further, I'm going to take off right here."

"Okay," said Mike, "we'll ride the next one to-gether."

Mickey and Mike paddled hard, and Mike actually paddled to the left, placing him in a ridiculously deep position. Together they caught the biggest wave they had ever seen. Mickey made it about half way to the bottom, hit a bump, flew into the air and then went down into darkness. After pushing up through the churning foam, he looked around to see if his board was anywhere in sight. It was not. Then he looked for Mike, who had also wiped out on that wave. And there was Mike, smiling, laughing, screaming near him. For a while the two friends sat in the water jacked up on adrenaline and screaming at the top of their lungs as their joy echoed through the bay.

Mickey went back home, and in time his mom forgave him for his untimely departure. He even went back to school where he found that things seemed different. He had not grown any, and was still unable to play varsity football or basketball. But now he carried something that he prized more than any letter on a sweater. He owned something that none of them would ever even attempt. Nobody knew why, but Mickey Muñoz walked the halls of Santa Monica High School a lot taller after that.

*Mickey Muñoz lives with his wife, Peggy, in San Juan Capistrano, California. He builds custom surfboards and boats and surfs whenever there's a swell.*

Waimea, the first day. Mickey Muñoz (top) and Mike Stange (bottom). Photo: Don James. 1957.

Comrades in arms. (left to right) Henry Preece, Greg
Noll and Buffalo Keaulana.

Greg Noll's hand. Rick James' thumb.
Photo: Laura Noll

Margo Godfrey winning her first World Contest at 14 years old. Puerto Rico. 1968. Photo: Leroy Grannis

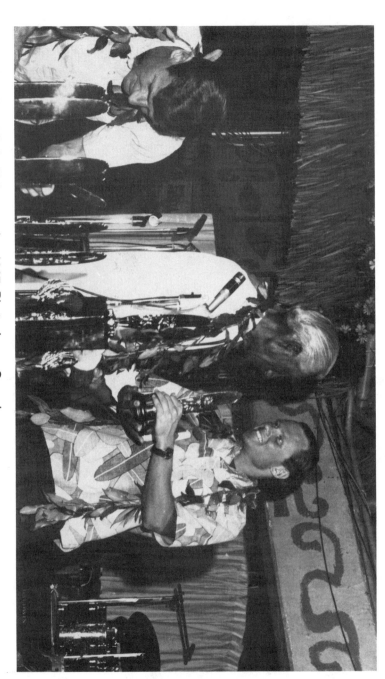

Corky Carroll and Duke Kahanamoku. 1967. Photo: Leroy Grannis

Makaha Quonset hut feast. Circa 1955. Photo: Don James

Phil Edwards and Buzzy Trent. Checking out big Waimea Bay. Circa 1960. Photo: Don James

Chris O'Rourke, with protective hockey helmet.

David Nuuhiwa, Pipeline. December, 1965. Photo: Leroy Grannis

Bob McTavish, Rincon. March, 1968. Photo: Leroy Grannis

Famous for surfing Pipeline as a goofy-foot, Butch Van Artsdalen was also known to charge big Waimea Bay as a regular-foot. December 1966. Photo: Leroy Grannis

# IN THE MAUI BUBBLE

*Nineteen-sixty-nine stands as the ultimate vintage year for surfers of my generation, the yardstick against which all other periods of surf are measured. In that time, I had the honor of living on Maui. It was the craziest year of my life, or maybe it was the sanest. Regardless, I doubt if anyone has ever ridden better waves than those which poured into Honolua Bay that December. Endless blue perfection was nearly all that mattered to any of us at the time.*

The retaining wall at Hookipa Park had been reduced to a pile of broken concrete and scattered boulders, and now the surf was attacking the pavilion perched at least ten feet above the beach. Raw Pacific power generated in the Aleutians pushed against the Islands, and I traced a line from as far out to sea as 20/20 vision would allow. The wave feathered and stood like a mountain, miles from shore, and then, not finding sufficient depth to break, it flattened out again. The cycle repeated many times, building and falling and tossing 30 foot plumes of spray into the air each time it peaked and the offshore wind ripped its top off. It jacked up taller still when it connected with a reef so far outside that none of the locals on hand knew of its existence. The wave began to break for real, this time in open ocean.

It fell slowly. Like a dream the wave fell, and I counted as the water dropped from top to bottom, and accomplished Hiroshima devastation, turning the air to fog. Paia, Pakakalo and

Kahului Harbor broke all size barriers. Maalaea was flat. So was Lahina.

No more waves showed until Rainbows, which was empty, double overhead and Velzyland perfect. But Honolua Bay was the destination. Molokai, close enough to touch, formed part of the frame of small wave window that allowed the swell of a lifetime to funnel in for our enjoyment and terror.

Taking the final curve, we saw the bay at full throttle. Five, six, seven, eight, nine power walls in a row peeled off like a tin roof in a typhoon.

The main players were Les Potts, Paul McKinney, Buddy Boy Kaohi, Herbie Torrens, Steve Dabney, Jackie Dunn and Charley Quisnel. Jock Sutherland and Billy Hamilton had not yet flown into town with John Severson, who was filming *"Pacific Vibrations."* By the time they arrived the surf had dropped and turned side-shore. Skidding into the red mud, we walked and slid to the cliff's edge. From there it looked immense, nearly twice as big as it really was. A young up-and-comer named Owl Chapman raced down the cliff with his new Brewer gun. Some struggled up the cliff empty handed after sacrificing their boards to the cave. Others went into the cave to find nothing more than foam and glass splinters. But some boards miraculously survived the pounding unscratched. Those who crawled to shore defeated were often covered with the blood of a pre-cord dance over the boulders.

Potts dropped in late on a huge set wave, hit the bottom, punched the tail, and rolled out hard and fast. Holding a high line, standing tall on his eight-foot pintail, he suddenly slinked down low and shifted his weight onto his back foot, his white hair flying like a flag as he raced against the fury of the bay, barely beating it to the bowl where he got deep.

I was green but knew something of Hawaiian etiquette. So, when asked how big the sets were, I replied conservatively, saying that they were 15 feet. The older guys laughed, shook their heads, and said maybe 12. I was embarrassed until the next year when I read in the magazines that the same guys were calling that day 20.

I paddled out on the first board that I had ever made. The purple thing had been hacked out with a saw and a rough file, cut down from a Hynson Red Fin to a 17-inch-wide, accidentally asymmetrical, three-stringered piece of crap that barely resembled a surfboard. I tested it and myself on the biggest waves of my life.

I sat out on the shoulder where nothing could swing wide and smash me. Paul McKinney, who had overheard my loud talk about being a big-wave rider in the warm flatness of Lahina's Animal Farm that summer, paddled over, looked squarely into my eyes and asked, "What's the matter boy, got butterflies in your stomach?" He laughed in my face and paddled away.

I flashed back to the safety of Animal Farm, Maui's halfway house for wayward surfers. Owl and Gary Chapman had lived there, and I was lucky to get their room when they left. The unlucky ones slept on the floor, or lived in tents. No matter, the rent was always the same, ten dollars a week. A group of us fresh from the mainland were sitting outside eating breakfast on a quiet, surfless morning, and bragging about how we were going to take apart the bay when it next broke. "You guys are nothing but a bunch of old women," shot McKinney. "You ever ride Sunset Beach?" His head was thrust confrontively toward me. I lowered my eyes as he climbed onto the wooden picnic table where we were eating. Cereal bowls chattered against the wood, and some bowls fell to the ground dumping oatmeal onto the grass as McKinney demonstrated a Sunset bottom turn while we reverently watched.

The sound of the next set brought me back to Honolua. I was still in the channel and McKinney was again taking off behind the peak and setting his edge for the long shot into the bowl. My God, he was going to die if he didn't make it. But he did make it, swinging hard off the bottom and throwing it up high into the lip, defying the power to knock him down, which it could not. When he paddled back out, I was still in the same spot, petrified and alone, and watching thick lines bend around Coconut Grove, the outside point. McKinney paddled by and looked back once to make sure that I knew he had seen me cowering in my hiding place.

I put my head down and paddled hard toward the pack. Thinking that it would be safer, I stroked inside and caught a smaller wave in front of someone. Because of the wave's power and my own fear, I had to rest my hands on my back leg to steady the long drop. I skidded to the bottom where I began a slow turn, and looked up, over my shoulder to the point where the top of the biggest wave I had ever ridden in California would have been. All I saw there was water.

The wave was not a small one after all, but one of the ones I had been warned about. The older guys had said that the most dangerous waves had an odd twist to them and would sometimes roll beyond the pack and then unloaded with twice the normal punch in shallower water.

The crappy board held through the turn, but rather than follow the natural projection toward the top, I steered a safer line along the bottom. The water opened up at the bowl into a tube so big that I couldn't tell if I was in it or not. I know now that I was not even close. But I was home free. I felt peaceful and strong until I looked up to see the fin of a green board turning directly above my head. McKinney! Where had he come from? Thinking that he was going to spin out and land on top of me, I panicked, jumped, went over the falls, and was pressed hard onto the rock bottom.

The wipeout was quick and fairly painless. I checked everything when I came up. No blood. No broken bones. Still breathing. Looking in, I saw that my board had been snapped clean in two and that the pieces were washing against the rocks. I was grateful that I would not have to go out again that day. Walking in, I picked up a few surface wounds which were numbed by happiness.

Some guys were patching their boards on the hood of a '50 Chevy with *"Bondo Fix A Dent."* Later I found out that's what everybody used when they were in a hurry to get back into the water. Somebody came by to ask me how big the surf was. I said 12 feet. I sat proudly next to my broken board with my legs crossed and spattered with my dried blood which I would not wipe off for anything in the world. An older guy with a long beard came over to offer me some Bondo. But when he noticed that the board had broken right on the picture of Jesus, which I had resined beneath the glass, he shook his head and said, "bad Karma," before walking away and leaving me empty handed and content not to have a board.

McKinney walked by dripping wet and gave me a smile that I first assumed to be sarcastic. This time I didn't back down from his powerful gaze, and watched as he gave a friendly nod before loading himself and his board into his car and driving back to Lahina.

I never did get another clear shot at big Honolua. It was always too crowded, onshore, something. There were other days at Pakakalo, the River Mouth, and inside Kahului Harbor. Outside harbor had huge waves that some people talked about riding. But it wasn't until the invention of cords that it became a somewhat regular surf spot.

The summer of '69 had been only fair. I spent it surfing Maui's Breakwall, Shark Pit, and Hookipa when everything else was flat. Rarely Maalaea, where I hit lucky once and found a solid four-foot swell running with only Herbie Fletcher and I out.

Herbie was riding the first down-railed surfboard that I had ever seen, a cool blade executed by Mike Hynson. We traded waves for a long time and he came close to doing the impossible, nearly making a couple of them. But he always got swatted down near the end. He rode the deepest tube that I had ever seen to that point, and I watched him fly behind the curtain as I paddle out. The wave held its shape but peeled too fast, and Herbie broke through the wall and straightened out at the last possible moment.

The motto for selling cars on Maui was, "If it makes it to the bay, it's okay." I owned the only car in our group, a rusted-shut '61 Ford Falcon wagon that died after a successful fruit run to Hana where Hunter tried to jump a puddle in the thing, and splashed down dead-center instead. Again, bad Karma, the all inclusive moral principle that guided our lives, had made sense of the disaster. After trying unsuccessfully to start the Falcon, we ended up "being mellow and releasing the vehicle to the earth," as Melanie, Hunter's hippie girlfriend, had said.

My brother Dave bought a '50 Ford for 50 dollars, and found out, during the 10,000 foot drop from Haleakala Crater, that it didn't have any brakes. Passing the blame for the car's condition back and forth, I thought we'd kill each other before we went over the cliff.

But we survived, barely squeaking into Lahina to find a few musicians from the popular '60s rock band, *Quicksilver Messenger Service*," jamming on the front lawn up the street from Animal Farm while some people fried in the sand. "Jeremiah The Preacher," a massive, bald headed man at least seven feet tall, walked up the beach when he heard the music. He had a voice equal to his great size, and a knowledge of books like the *Bhagavad-Gita*, which gave him further authority with us. He spoke to us about the impending doom soon to be unleashed against Maui if it did not repent of its folly. I listened attentively for a while but was torn between repentance and folly when two girls removed their tops and began swaying seductively on the lawn near me.

We were afraid to believe, and afraid not to believe. After all, Jeremiah had told my friend Ed that he would be eaten by a shark; and the very next day Ed was chased from the water by a big-finned creature at Maalaea. After that Jeremiah attracted a small following including his tiny girlfriend whom he called "The Daughter Of Egypt," saying that she was the reincarnation of the same woman of Biblical fame. He had little trouble convincing a small portion of the psychedelicized population of Maui that he was a prophet. I heard that his reign ended abruptly when a group of his disciples followed him to their deaths after he walked off of a tall cliff where they had been praying with their eyes closed.

We moved to Paia, into a three bedroom house that was infested with as many as 12 surfers at a time. One day a surf star wearing nothing but a loincloth entered without knocking. He immediately stripped down to nothing, sat on the cloth he had been wearing, and crossed himself into a full lotus position. Then he began preaching to us. I had seen magazine pictures and films of this diminished giant. Still young enough for hero worship, I hung on his every word. He explained Karma and the sacrament, his name for psychedelics, and the cosmic flow that moved all things from the flying saucers in the crater, to the swells of Honolua Bay. His hair and beard were long and knotted, his famine-thin body was covered with staph sores. I asked him what had happened to him and he replied like a parent who had abandoned the house to teenage sons for the weekend. "I left my body for three days, and when I got back it looked like this!" he said in disgust while lifting his withered arm for our inspection. Others of lesser fame, and similar mentality, came and went from our house.

Hendrix played the music. Brewer made the boards. Jock Sutherland was the man. Sutherland had picked up a hitchhiking friend of mine in Kahului, and scared the crap out of him by closing his eyes on the way through the tunnel on the way to Lahina. This, Sutherland later explained to him, was an exercise that he used to increase mental control. I guess it worked. Jock had astounding mental and physical control. He would side-slip down the face on big waves at the bay, and pull into the bowl time after time. There was a machine-like commando quality to him that still remains mysterious to me. He was this wave riding genius. Pure function, not great form. No hesitation. Always in the right spot. Maybe it came from being raised by a woman who is said to have swam around a large portion of Kauai with Joey Cabell in her middle age.

After the first of the massive north swells flattened the North Shore of Oahu, Maui became a surfer's refuge center. Knowing that Honolua would be all-time, and with nowhere else to go, a lot of new people came to town. I spoke with two hippies who said that they had been sitting in their house on Kam Highway when they heard something rumble at the door. One of them got up, opened the door and found that the house, which had always faced the ocean, was now facing the street and being pushed onto the road.

Maui was soon packed with some of the world's best surfers. For weeks they rewrote the book on Honolua Bay. Then one day, it just kind of quit breaking and everyone went home.

I moved for a time into the hill country of Haiku. Up the street from me, two formerly hot surfers, Chris Green and Chris Butler, known as Si Young, had started a very strict Zen monastery. They awoke each morning at 3:30, meditated for an hour and tended an organic vegetable garden. They ate tiny amounts of food, read only spiritual books, and meditated some more. They often vowed silence, but when Green was speaking I had some good talks with him about surfing and living naturally. Inspired by him, I shut off my electricity and water, and lived as close to the earth as possible. I fasted myself down to nothing and, like most Mauians of the time, fed an insatiable appetite for things spiritual with books like the Gita and eventually the Bible.

It was a hard, simple life, and before long it drove me crazy. It took half a day just to wash clothes in the creek. I had slipped out of surfing almost entirely, and was so isolated that I had passed my 21st birthday alone without even knowing which day it was.

That's when I moved into a house in Pakakalo with a couple of musicians. Music was a pretty big deal. World news was not. I didn't know anyone with a TV or a newspaper subscription, and I didn't hear about Woodstock or anybody walking on the moon for at least a year after they happened. Or, if I did hear about those things, they registered with less impact than the price of mangoes. We had no idea what was happening beyond our little group on Maui. I didn't know. I didn't care. And I was completely happy. Life then was directed by some very basic needs, not the least of which was surfing.

I guess that each generation has their year, and mine owns 1969. The swells will come up again, and Honolua will roar to life with waves of equal size. New heros will ride those waves better than the old heros. They will be attached by cords to far better boards than we had. And it will be great. But it won't be the same, because it won't be the same world that we knew then.

*

# THE GREAT WHITE WHALE

In 1965 Bob and Freddy Zerbie, twin brothers, lived in East Los Angeles, and felt a desperate need for liberation from that place. That's when they heard that Eddie Rivera's '32 Model B Ford was for sale, a car with a reputation equal to Rivera's own, a car which had nearly outrun the cops, until Eddie, who was drunk on a combination of *Colt .45 Malt Liquor, Aqua Velva After Shave, and Romalar Cough Syrup*, tried to jump a drainage ditch in the wagon, but landed instead in muddy water, up to the fur dice on his rearview mirror.

Bob and Freddy went to visit the car at the Rivera house, and when Mrs. Rivera answered the door, Bob asked for Eddie. "Eddie is away, visiting his Aunt in Sacramento," she said, offering the standard excuse she used each time her son was locked up in juvenile hall.

The woman swung the door back in preparation of slamming it in Bob's big, round face until he asked, "Does he want to sell his car?" Mrs. Riviera hesitated, opened the door a little wider and peered out at the rusting hunk robbing her of her driveway. She glared meanly at the car for a moment, then she snapped around angrily to face Bob. "Give me a hundred bucks and it's yours," she said, pecking her open hand with her index finger. With that, she made a shooing motion to Bob and Freddy and the car, repeating the words "A hundred bucks," before disappearing behind the slammed wooden door.

Barely able to imagine a hundred bucks in one place, the boys, nonetheless, cut lawns, collected bottles, withdrew every cent from their two digit savings accounts, and picked oranges from the neighbor's trees and sold them back to them. Finally they scrapped together $67.79. They took the offering to Mrs. Rivera and she agreed to let them have the car after they worked off the remaining $32.21.

Four weekends in a row the boys pulled weeds, trimmed bushes, cut lawns, and hauled scrap iron from the Rivera yard in the red Western Flyer wagon that they had owned since December 25, 1954. When the final payment was made, Mrs. Rivera handed over the keys and the pink slip and dusted off her hands before sealing herself within the old house again.

Bob, who had just turned 16 and achieved a driver's license only three days earlier, drove nervously and slowly to their house, somehow hitting every pothole in the road as they sputtered, all smiles, and parked in the Zerbie driveway next to piles of mud encrusted hubcaps, dented car fenders, and other crap which old man Zerbie had jealously hovered over for the last 30 years.

Even before the car cooled down, they had lifted the hood and attacked the engine with pliers and screwdrivers, removing the metal thing, which they thought was the carburetor, and taking it apart, until it lay in pieces, scattered all over the driveway. They scrubbed all of the parts with Ajax, reassembled most of them, and were stoked when the car ran only slightly worse than it had before. It still sputtered and stammered, but now it backfired loudly whenever Bob let off the gas. The boys loved that sound, and it somehow reminded them of the spurting of a whale. And so the car became known to them, and to everyone else in town, as "The Great White Whale," even though it was not white.

Having heard about good surf in Mexico, they wanted to go and get some of it. Bob practiced for Mexico by driving in the alley behind the house while Freddy rode behind him on a metal-wheeled skateboard. Freddy held a rope which was attached to the Zerbie Great Dane, King. Bob would drive and King would chase the car, biting at the tires and running as fast as he could, which was very fast. When Bob reached exactly 20 miles per hour, he would slam on the brakes and King would swerve around the car. Freddy, however, was much slower than King, and slammed into the back doors of the Whale while Bob laughed hysterically. Freddy vowed revenge on Bob, but since he never got hurt, he continued riding the skateboard behind the car, behind King, until Bob hit the brakes and Freddy piled into the rear doors again. Freddy's vow for revenge against his brother completed the cycle, which continued for two weeks, until the tires went bald.

With no map, six cans of Campbell's Soup, a loaf of bread, a Coleman Stove, two sleeping bags, two surfboards, and a box of paraffin wax the boys rolled south to Mexico, sure that it was somewhere near the end of the freeway, which it was. Once beyond the Tijuana maze, they drove over the hills, past graves marked with candles and statues of saints, into the dark of a Friday night where Bob flew off the road and straight over a steep cliff.

Thinking that they were about to die, Freddy took his revenge by pulling Bob's hair, with both hands, as hard as he could. The Whale flew in the dark as Freddy held onto Bob's hair while praying that he and Bob would go to heaven. They flew only a few feet, until they were jerked to a hard stop and rolled themselves up beneath the dashboard, to shield themselves from the death that never came. They uncovered their eyes to see the headlights shining upon a gigantic boulder, the only visible rock on the entire cliff. There they sat, balanced delicately, about 100 feet above a sheer cliff and certain death. Freddy crossed himself as they tiptoed out the door, and the Whale rocked and creaked and threatened to dislodge from its delicate perch, and fall into the abyss. Back up on the road, Freddy flagged down the first truck he saw. The driver felt sorry for the boys and refused the money they offered, but did not have, for towing them off the hill.

The Whale had survived with nothing but a bent front bumper and a small dent in the hood. Freddy picked wildflowers and placed them on the side of the road as an offering to God, before Bob drove, without further mishap, into the night. When he became too sleepy to drive, Bob pulled over. Expecting to rest for only a moment, the brothers did not wake until the sun opened their eyes. Before them was the miracle of perfect four foot waves, peeling into a small bay with nobody around.

The next weekend they went to Mexico again, and again they drove, without plan or map, until they slept on the side of the road. Then they were greeted by perfect five foot peaks, miles from the spot they had found last week.

From then on they pointed the Whale north or south and miraculously found waves wherever they went. Anytime, anywhere, when Bob and Freddy arrived, the waves always got good, the best they had been in months. And the car, with its expired registration and blown muffler, seemed invisible to cops, who never once glanced at them as they moved up and down the coast, or across the boarder, into Baja.

Freddy hung a crucifix from the car's rear-view mirror, and prayed that it would continue to be blessed. He gave thanks that the tires never wore out, and that they never ran out of gas although the needle hovered near empty most of the time.

Although it was not a pretty thing, Bob and Freddy loved the Whale dearly. They would save their lunch money until they had a few dollars for presents, then, as if competing for the affections of the same girl, each would try to outdo the other. Freddy bought a can of spray paint for the rims, Bob bought a head-rest for the driver's seat. When Freddy bought a blanket to cover the hole in the passenger seat, Bob bought a can of oil to replace the two which had leaked out. Through all of this adoration, the Whale stayed impartial, and treated both brothers equally well.

Weird Denny Carnahan was a senior when Bob and Freddy were sophomores. Denny, who had been going to Mexico for five years told the boys about lonely points as good as Malibu. The stories so hypnotized Bob that he offered Denny a ride to Mexico in exchange for his knowledge. The pious Freddy, who was unmoved by Carnahan's tales asked Bob, "What if the blessing is only good for the two of us, and Weird Denny brings no blessing of his own to the Whale?"

Flicking the crucifix on the mirror with his index finger, Bob spoke, "We've been lucky so far, but Denny will show us to the best surf in Baja, blessing or none." Freddy was worried because Bob had flicked the crucifix and also because Weird Denny had achieved his name by setting his school books on fire in a classroom. Freddy thought for a moment and then countered Bob's logic with better logic.

"The Whale will get us anywhere if we are good, and continue to pray," he said. Until recently Bob would not dispute this, but now his psychology teacher had nearly erased his faith, and was making it seem irrational. Bob flicked the crucifix a little harder. "Don't be irrational Freddy," said Bob, trying to sound all-wise, like his teacher did. Freddy did not like the word irrational any more than Bob did, and so he kept quiet about Denny.

On day one, the trio passed the spots Bob and Freddy had found on their own. Where there had been good surf before, the waves this day were flat. Denny was unruffled, however, saying that his spot always had good waves. On the morning of day two, Denny was looking confused. By that afternoon he pulled a bottle from beneath the front seat, unscrewed the metal cap and took a long drink. Freddy felt sick and watched helplessly as the senior became very drunk. Freddy mentioned that they had always found good surf before. He was not trying to offend Denny by saying this, but to help Bob realize that the blessings had indeed departed the Whale. Denny, who was riding shotgun in the front seat, turned around to Freddy who sat on a pile of blankets and sleeping bags behind him. With a drunken smile he said, "When a car has lost its magic, it needs to be sacrificed." Bob was concentrating on his driving and didn't seem to notice the words. Denny slumped low in his seat and continued to drink. Freddy prayed and worried silently.

Valiantly, the Whale handled the rocks and the washed-out road. Freddy watched the gas needle fall quickly toward empty, wondering if the Whale was under a curse instead of a blessing now, and if they would soon run out of gas. Denny propped his head up in time to point Bob down a dirt road, and they bounced for miles over the rutted path until they came upon a long, sandy beach with small rights breaking off of a sandbar. Tired from the long drive, Bob and Freddy paddled out immediately. Denny sat in the car, watching the brothers while drinking from the bottle.

Freddy found a decent wave and rode it to the beach. After wiping out on a small right, Bob sat alone and discouraged in the lineup, thinking about looking for lefts. That's when he saw the Whale crawling backwards, up along the road. "He's ditching us!" shouted Freddy as he paddled back out toward Bob. The car continued in reverse up the road as Bob began to paddle in furiously. Then the Ford lunged forward, dust pouring from the wheels like fire as it moved quickly toward the sand berm. Gaining speed, the Whale jerked, and bumped and lumbered on, toward the water.

Denny must have been doing 60 when he left the ground and sat, suspended in the Whale, in the air, for what seemed like minutes. When the Whale finally landed, it bounced down onto the hard sand, and continued moving until the car was up to the windows in water.

Bob and Freddy ran over to the sinking Whale, and opened the door to retrieve Denny, who rescued his bottle before leaving the car. Bob punched Denny in his stupid-looking face as

Denny stood laughing with a small line of blood running down his mouth, saying, "Hey, Bob, mellow out, man. I did it for you. When the tide comes up and covers the car it will make a reef and you'll have perfect lefts to yourself out there."

The tide did come up, and it swallowed the Whale, but no lefts appeared above it. Somehow Bob was unable to comprehend Denny's selfless action, and he remained mad at Denny all that night as the three surfers tramped back to the main road, and then hitchhiked into Ensenada where they caught a bus to San Diego. By San Diego, Denny was sober and hung over. There he called his brother to come and pick them up.

Denny's brother, Andy, arrived hours later in a beaten up '54 Ford wagon. As they headed back home, the car sputtered just as the Whale had always done. When the car backfired, Bob's eyes filled up with love, and he contemplated the beauty of the Ford while stroking its worn upholstery softly. " How would you like to sell this thing,"? asked Bob.

With Bob as its pilot, and Freddy as its spiritual protector, "Whale Two," became a legend in our town.

✳

# MAGIC SAM or, THE TELEPATHIC LEG ROPE

There were no sponsorships for Nat Young when he grew up in the Sydney suburb of Collaroy. And so, like most Aussie surfers of his day, he surfed on whatever he could find and learned to like it. The board that he came to prominence on was named "Sam," and Nat considered it an old friend. In the States we had heard about Nat and Sam, some saying that they were the best one-two punch since Phil and his board, "Baby."

Legend has it that Sam was really nothing more than a pile of rotten balsa and patched dings. It had apparently been cut down to 9'2", and the fin was ground down into a speed shape to keep up with the times. The advantage of such a board is that you come to know it very well. Nat Young did impossible moves on that board, moves that would even stoke his hero, Phil Edwards.

But some say that it was Sam that made Nat so good. The board went beyond natural laws, and possessed a vague mystical quality, they say. According to legend, when Nat lost his board he would call out "Sam!" and the board would stop like a well-trained dog, dead in the water, until its master swam over to retrieve it.

✱

# BOB WOULD GO

*In the mid-1960s Bob McTavish helped to pioneer
a new movement in surfing called "The Shortboard
Revolution." A few years later he had faded from
the limelight, and moved to the country to make
surfboards and raise a family. One of the best
Australian surfers in his prime, he had become a
weekend warrior. His wife's cheesecake didn't
help matters any.*

Bob McTavish was a few years past his prime,
ready to surf, but out of shape when he landed on
Oahu with the intention of riding the North
Shore for the first time in years. Sunset Beach
was good and big—a solid 12 foot with bigger
sets, some of which nearly closed out the channel
as they thundered in from the northwest.

That was okay, he could sit wide for a
while and watch the waves—maybe ease into the
less critical ones if he wanted to. Or, if he didn't
want to, he could just paddle out and watch from
deep water on this, his first day at Sunset in over
a decade.

But something happened that day that
always happens to Bob McTavish types. Enthu-
siasm got the best of him, and he paddled right
into the pack of 40 or 50 of the best surfers in the
world. Nobody there knew him, but he recognized some in the pack from magazines. This
was the new guard. He looked for a familiar face
and found only one, a good one to know, someone
who dominated, taking off deep, behind everyone else and pulling into treacherous high lines.

This was a man whom Bob had met years
earlier in Hawaii, the legendary Eddie Aikau.
Mac sat out two sets, sitting high at the crest and
looking down, deep into the trough. He won-

dered if his soft body could take the pounding if he didn't make the drop. It was big and steep and dangerous. This would be a good learning experience and a time to relearn the old tricks that Sunset always threw at you.

The waves were beautiful and even more powerful than he had remembered them. Everyone but Eddie surfed cautiously, hesitantly, letting the biggest waves roll beneath them.

A big wall of water choked off Backyards and the pack knew that a set was moving toward Sunset. The set stood up far out at sea, capped and rolled and nearly broke as everyone paddled for the channel that would hopefully not close out. In their panic, some paddled hard toward shore. Bob paddled out and over a step-ladder set of waves that had gone from eight, to ten, to twelve, and now threatened to get bigger.

The set poured through, and Bob watched everyone pull back as the waves hedged on close-out size. Minutes after the set had passed he looked around. Fear cut through him. Most everyone had been swept from the lineup. Did they know something he didn't? Would Sunset close out on him like it had in the mid-'60s when he paddled straight out to sea forever as the ocean erupted on him and Bobby Cloutier?

He looked to the half-dozen left in the lineup. Most looked fearful, all except for Eddie Aikau, who until then, had been focused in deep concentration on the demanding surf. Now, for the first time that day his features turned friendly. There was a smile as old memories built long ago came back. Memories, too, flooded McTavish's already overloaded brain. Eddie had been a young, wild kid charging the North Shore when Bob, the young Aussie rebel, first met him.

"Howzit Mac?" the powerful Hawaiian shouted above the raw sounds of the elements.

This was cool. Bob had just been acknowledged by the heaviest local in the water. Nobody would hassle him for waves now. Not that it mattered; he was not planning on taking any waves from where he sat. But he felt much better about being out there, and he had a feeling of increased confidence as he paddled over near Eddie and returned the friendly greeting. The others now looked at Bob, and wondered who the Australian friend of Eddie's was. Someone put the accent and the nickname, Mac, together, and soon the little group buzzed with the name Bob McTavish. They had all heard of him, the general of the shortboard revolution who had suffered equipment failure when the wrong board was sent to Sunset Beach, and the too wide vee-bottom spun out. Conversation was cut short when another big set swung in from the west, breathing hard down the necks of the anxious crowd. Bob figured that he would paddle out, and then over where he could watch Eddie from the safety of the channel.

He followed Eddie into position, and then began to stroke wide in order to get away from the intensity that had been emotionally pounding him for over an hour. He hadn't gone far when he heard it loud and clear. Words that would be welcomed at nearly any other surf spot in the world hit him like a slap in the face. Eddie had shouted an edict to the submissive crew as a massive wedge made its final approach.

"Okay, this one's Bob's. Nobody else go," the Hawaiian generously proclaimed.

"What could I do?" asked Bob of me as he told the story. "When Eddie Aikau says go, you go."

★

104

# BOB GOES

By-Bob McTavish

We've all heard tales of Dickie Cross; how he was caught outside in massive Sunset Beach in the late '50s, and how he paddled to Waimea and died trying to make it to shore. I went through the first part of that nightmare in December of 1967.

I was sharing a house at Gas Chambers with Mike Hynson and Mickey Dora. The surf was small, and so we body surfed fun two to three foot Rocky Point with Mike Doyle that morning. A new swell began to indicate at about 10 am. By midday we were waxing up for eight foot Sunset. By one o'clock, a couple of true sets hit the peak. By two o'clock we were into solid, 12 foot Sunset. It was coming up fast.

At about two-thirty the crowd was getting big, and all the well-known big wave riders were out: Rusty Miller, Greg Noll, Bob Shepherd, Jose Angel, Eddie and Clyde Aikau. At three o'clock, a monster set came wheeling in over the reef and swung way out towards the rip. All 50 of the guys in the water streaked towards the rip and out, except for me and Bobby Cloutier. The sets poured down on all of them as Bobby and I escaped over the top. We paddled out and around, towards Back Yards, and then, after the sets cleared, we looked to see forty-some grinning, bobbing heads, laughing in the whitewater, and moving slowly toward shore. Hoots and hollers filled the bay. It was getting big, and everyone felt it. That set nearly closed out on us. It was 15, 16, 17 feet and rising!

But we couldn't gloat on our victory of

making outside for long. Further outside was another set. Bigger. So we continued paddling out past Back Yards. That was the last we saw of any other surfers in the water that day. From three o'clock onwards, Bobby and I were the only two guys out at Sunset, because no one else could get out. The sets continued to pour in. Out at sea, Bobby and I went through an hour and a half of paddling at a constant, steady rate. Up huge faces we stroked, and as we busted the lip we'd get a glimpse of endless lines of waves moving in. Behind each wave was a bigger one. We'd drop down the back, the rain from the offshore pouring over us, blinding us, just paddling hard to get over the next wave. This process was repeated a hundred times.

You'd think we would have paddled out to sea a mile or so. No. The constant shoreward motion of these 20-foot-plus sets kept us fairly close to the break, only about twice as far out as the regular Sunset lineup.

It was about 4:30 when Bobby, who was 100 yards further out than I was, whirled his board around and paddled into a perfect 25-foot wave. He plummeted down the face, and then casually pivoted a backside turn. Then this 25-foot mongrel poured around him. From my position paddling up the face, he looked like he was inside of a 25 foot barrel, but he was probably just in the mouth of the beast.

As he kicked out, I hooted and told him that I couldn't believe the size of that thing he'd just ridden. He didn't have time to reply; we needed to continue our steady paddle out.

The sun was gone by 5 o'clock and Bobby pointed out to me that "When it gets this big, this fast, you always get some long lulls. When one hits," he said, "paddle like hell for shore." Sure enough, at about 10 past 5, we paddled over yet another huge wall but the lines out to sea, instead of being endlessly stacked as they had been for the last two hours, were tapering. Usually at this time of night the lines look bigger after the sun has set. But no! The swell had dropped off. This was the lull we were waiting for.

Bobby and I started our mad scramble back towards the beach. We raced in, knowing that the swell would soon be pounding down upon us again. Within ten 10 minutes we were back into the proper Sunset lineup. It was dark. No one was visible on the beach when the first of the big sets returned. I lost contact with Bobby at this point. As I approached the normal Sunset take off point a huge mass of white water broke behind me in the dark. All I could do was hold onto my rails in a prone position and hope to ride out the whitewater blast. I couldn't hold on, however, and my board was wrenched from my hands. After that I was twisted and hurled and worked in the blackness.

But I had been worked a thousand times before, and so I kept calm and gradually rose to the surface, knowing that I'd been transported a long way in by the explosive whitewater. The next couple of waves finished the job of pushing me toward shore. I was in far enough now to ride out the diminished push of the two waves, and I was dropped into the Sunset in-shore rip.

I knew that I had to get across the rip to the beach before the water rushed back out through the main vent, carrying millions of tons of water back out to sea and me along with it. I swam like crazy across the rip and then finally clawed my way up onto the sand. Stoked!

Someone had found my board and stuck the nose up, in the sand, but there was nobody around. No one. None of my mates. Not Russell, not Hynson, not Doyle. All of those guys who had been wiped out nearly three hours before were gone. Not even the guy who had found my board, and placed it in the sand like a grave marker was there. And where was Bobby? All I know is that he too lived to tell this story.

*

# BOB GOES UPSIDE DOWN

Bob McTavish is a visionary. And, like most visionaries, he's never satisfied. With anything. He tinkers with stuff, changes it, redesigns it, and puts it back together in a way that is often unrecognizable. That's what drove him as the general of the "shortboard revolution" in the mid-'60s, and that's what drives him today.

By 1967 McTavish was already bored with the bottom to top turning of the radical short, deep vee-bottomed boards he had invented. The first of that line was a nine-footer with a long, deep vee. He rode that board from sunup to sundown one day and one day only. That's all he needed to figure out the design flaws. The next day he made a new board and never surfed the nine-footer again. After that he made an 8'6". Within a month he was down to 7'6".

He was burning to break free from the constraints of straight-line surfing. In his quest for freedom he envisioned things like aerials, ten years before anyone actually accomplished them.

There's no doubt that Bob was physically and mentally capable of air at that time. Only his equipment held him back. But Bob was not really looking to do aerials, but something else, something which no stand-up surfer had ever done. Bob McTavish wanted to look up at his feet and to surf upside down. To this end he was dedicated, but he was one of the few people to believe that inversion was possible.

Moving to California for a time, McTavish began to redefine surfboards in a way that upset many traditionalists. He had abandoned noseriding nearly entirely, and was concentrating on the tube, fast turns and hard, in the pocket momentum. Rincon was his favorite U.S. test tank, and '68 was a vintage year.

After surfing Rincon all day, McTavish would go home, lie down in the top bunk of his friend's house, and put his feet onto the ceiling. There he would lay, concentrating on one split second in time, visualizing surfing upside down. The owner of the house would often interrupt Bob in his surf-inspired meditation, and ask him what he was doing, to which Bob would give an involved response about how surfing in a straight line was dull, and that given the right wave, a surfer could break from that line and go upside down. While impressed with Bob's surfing, the home owner was skeptical. "Upside down, huh? Well, good luck."

But Bob was not deterred by skepticism, and each evening when the man came home he would find Bob, lying on the bunk bed, feet on the ceiling, eyes closed, imagining that he was surfing with his feet above his head. He'd just shake his head and walk out.

Rincon was host to a good swell and all the boys were there—Aaberg, Yater, Greenough, and the foreigner, McTavish. Greenough, who was the undisputed fastest man on water in those days, rode from the indicator into the cove, carving, hitting the top and getting barreled through entire sections. When McTavish attempted to follow Greenough's lead, he usually got swatted down by a connecting section before making it around the corner. But Bob would not give up. He would never give up.

The noseriders were out at the cove. The gliders held position at the point, and the speed surfers, led by Greenough, penetrated Indicator.

A six-foot set marched through. Greenough, who's "spoon" was more glass than foam, sat low in the water. Catching the first wave, he drove off the bottom from behind the wall, turned up into the tube, and then cut back hard, moving faster and faster from top to bottom all the way through to the point where he pulled over the top as the section collapsed in front of him.

McTavish, who was not about to let some 'Sepo' steal the day, was wound tight with adrenaline. Bob paddled into the second wave, forced a hard line to the bottom, and, shifting his weight, pulled a tight and hard turn which sent him to the top, and "Bang." He hit it hard. Then he drove back into the pit, swung off the bottom and again exploded off the top. He was moving fast now, and he linked up several more hard turns, gaining speed with each one, feeling the power surge through his board as it flexed beneath him and then moved electrically through his body. Two others looked to drop in, and "Bam," Bob took the top off of the section. With increased speed, he proceeded to ride close to the hook as the wave lined up all the way to Oil Piers.

It was several seconds before the wave peeled slowly enough to allow Bob to go to the bottom and turn again. The turn was of the hard, on-rail variety and generated still more speed. It had been the perfect ride, and he was only about half way through. All he had to do was stand there, and he could have scored straight tens on any judges score sheet if this had been a contest. The contest for him was not to be the best status quo mannequin, but to break down the walls that had kept surfing stagnant for so long. Determined to destroy that wall, he recoiled, pressed off the bottom and hit the top again. He moved now at high speed, watching surfers' bent expressions of awe and wonder as he flew beyond the first section of the point.

The wave was still well overhead when Bob tightened himself for the next section. It was now or never. Squaring off the bottom, he felt the vee hit capacity and approach the spin-out point. He redirected the board up onto the ceiling for another perfect off the top. Of course, he had it made. He was feeling strong now. Invincible! Then, like a dream, like in his vision, he moved into the zone, holding position for what seemed like minutes. Instead of hitting off the top with his inside rail, and directing his board back down, however, he freed his rail, kept the pressure on it, double pumped and turned up until he was vertical with the lip. Not content to do the best off the lip the world had ever seen, he ignored the hoots of the crowd and pushed further, spinning the board up against the roof of the wave. He looked up, and for the first time he saw his feet above him, and water being separated by the board as the vee stuck fast. He hung upside down like a bat. It couldn't be, but it was. He was frozen there for an indeterminable amount of time, and he could see everything around himself clearly. As time sped up again, those in the water became a blurry picket fence of celebration. Bob continued to red line it to the inside.

McTavish freed his rail and swung his board back around and into trim. Then he pushed the board hard to avoid the falling section, and raced to the bottom, barely beating the whitewater down. He squared into another turn, and raced to the inside section. The wave walled up perfectly for him without anyone anywhere near the shoulder. Nobody would dare to drop in now.

He was in the cove, trimming fast in the hook, letting the wave break submissively onto his shoulders as those who had witnessed the ride cheered loudly.

He rode that wave into the sand, and stepped off on the beach. As he ran back to the point, the boys on the beach could see that Bob McTavish was not only smiling broadly. He looked satisfied. Finally.

*

*Bob McTavish lives with his family in Lenox Heads, Australia. He continues to build advanced surfboards, and dreams of making them do incredible things.*

## MISTER MAC, METAL SHOP TEACHER

Mister Mac loved things made out of steel. In fact, I am convinced that he felt that most things should have been metallic. It suited his futuristic late-'50s vision, where he and people like him envisioned a shiny, reflective rust-free planet.

He himself seemed to be made of hard alloys. His voice resonated like Big Ben. His flat-top with fenders swept back reminded me of a Cadillac. He wore a big watch with a metal watchband, a metal tieclip, metal cuff links and had chrome buckles on his shoes.

And there was nothing he could not build out of metal: tool boxes, filing cabinets, toys, and weird sculptors with people welded into strange shapes.

He had heard that some of us in class were beginning to surf, and picked me out to tell the class about surfboard construction. "A surfboard is made of a foam core, with a wooden stringer and then covered with fiberglass," I told the class. Nobody really cared, they just sat there, most of them wondering what fiberglass was. But Mister Mac had a smirk on his face. "Do they ever break?" He asked me."

"Yes, sometimes they break," I replied.

"Well, they should be made of metal," he said predictably.

"Metal would be too heavy," I replied.

"No dumb-dumb, you hollow it out; have you ever seen a ship?"

The class laughed at me, and I had no reply. I went back to work on my tool box, and wondered about a metal surfboard.

Over the next few months, Mister Mac

began to work on a massive project. First he brought in large strips of sheet metal. Then he cut the strips into the shape of a surfboard. He heated up the two halves, and somehow bent them so that they were convex. Next he riveted sides onto the board, and then welded the entire thing together. Finally he affixed a thick metal fin to the board, and then proudly displayed the strange-looking vehicle before the class.

His smirk had grown to the full extent of his mouth when he called me forward to hold the new board. I had to admit to myself that it was cool looking, but it bothered me when Mister Mac said "Men, I give you the surfboard of the future." I tried to pick it up, but it seemed to weigh over 100 pounds. Plus it was too wide to hold under your arm. I couldn't say anything to Mister Mac, so I just went back to my work station, and let him have his moment of glory.

That weekend I went surfing as usual. On Monday, when I returned to school, there was Mister Mac as usual, but wearing a bandage on his forehead, and looking very unsure of himself. My friend later told me that he had heard that Mister Mac's surfboard had been a failure, and that he had nearly killed himself trying to ride it at Huntington Pier. I wished that I could have seen him try to surf.

For a moment I daydreamed of myself shooting the pier as Mister Mac paddled out on his metal barge. I saw him take off and pearl, before I paddled over and saved him from drowning. I was snapped back to reality by the stiff snap of a wooden pointer against the blackboard.

"Sometimes, said Mister Mac, we need to combine elements. I have taken a first step in inventing the metal surfboard, and after testing the board I know what I need to do. I will now make a surfboard with the standard materials: foam, and fiberglass," he said looking at me. Still looking my direction he asked, "Have I left anything out?"

"Yes, I replied, the wooden stringer."

"No, I will not use a wooden stringer; I'm going to use a metal one," Mister Mac announced proudly.

That sounded reasonable to me, so I didn't say anything, but once again returned to my work station while Mister Mac gave me a triumphant look.

Over the next month his board took shape. He bought a nice blank, cut the wood out of it, glued up a metal stringer, and spent the next two weeks trying to shape the thing into something that looked like a surfboard. Being a master craftsman the board eventually took shape, and was glassed to perfection. Then he painted a picture on the deck of a bar of steel being melted in a furnace. To the board he attached the metal skeg from the solid metal surfboard. I had to admit that this board looked pretty nice, and when I picked it up, it was only a little heavier than my Hobie.

The next day I brought a box of paraffin wax to school with the intention of showing Mister Mac how to wax his new board. He looked at the wax, and asked me how to apply it. "Well, there's three ways, you can either rub it on slowly, melt it in a pan and drip it on, or use a paint brush to put it on."

"Nope, too slow," said Mister Mac arrogantly. He then took a bar of wax and laid it on the deck of his new board. After that he took a blowtorch, and approached the wax. "Mister Mac, " I screamed in protest, "You're going to ruin your board if you do that." He just looked at me as if to say that I didn't know anything, and after all the things he'd done I figured he was right. He brought the torch down toward the board and turned up the flame. Suddenly the board started to smoke. Mister Mac had really screwed up, and he knew it. But he was too committed to this project to admit it, and so he just kept the flame turned toward the wax. The wax melted and flowed all over the board and onto the floor, and the fiberglass caught fire. Still Mister Mac kept the torch on the board. We all looked, amazed that he was burning up the board.

When he had finally burned a deep hole into the foam, Mister Mac took off his welding goggles, turned off the torch, and addressed the class. "Now, did you learn anything at all from that little experiment, "he said, scowling at me. I was stunned, the poor guy had just destroyed his surfboard, and was trying to turn it into a lesson. "No, I don't think so," I said, feeling a little sorry for the man. "Always use metal," he said. "For everything!" He put the board into a corner where it stayed all that school year. The man was really something. He really hated anything made of plastic.

✳

# BUS FULL OF DREAMS

It was Christmas Eve and Greg Noll was having a little party at his surf shop in Hermosa Beach. He had already downed a couple of strong drinks, and was in rare form when his friend, big-wave rider, Kit Horn, strolled in. Noll, who is always up for a practical joke, began to improvise a new training method for riding big waves, something which fascinated Horn. Lunada Bay, the miniature Waimea Bay of Southern California, was big when Noll baited Horn. The following is Noll's account of that night.

*"At the shop we got to drinking wine. Kit Horn wasn't a big drinker and was talking about Lunada Bay which was breaking at about 15 feet. By this time it was about three in the afternoon and we were getting pretty hammered. I told Kit that I had a special workout for getting in shape for big waves. 'What you did,' I said, 'was tie yourself into a big truck tire inner tube, paddle out at Lunada Bay, get yourself right in the impact zone, then try to catch a wave backwards. There with your wine bottle and your inner tube you drink and wait for a wave to break on you. If you lose your bottle of wine or you quit drinking, you're automatically disqualified.'*

*" ... We paddled out in our tubes and sat right in the impact zone. A 15 foot set comes through and pounds both of us. We're laughing anyway, having a great time. Kit loses his inner tube but holds onto his bottle. I'm getting a little concerned about him, but he just laughs..."*
—From *DA BULL, Life Over The Edge.*

Henry Preece has probably suffered more

of Greg Noll's pranks than any man alive. And yet, Henry remains one of Greg's best friends. Henry was one of the most important surf pioneers on the North Shore of Oahu in the '50s. While his contribution was apparently unintentional, he was the first person ever to surf Haleiwa in modern times. As the story goes, Henry was chased from his home on Oahu's West Side, to the North Shore, after jilting a girl who's brothers wanted to kill him. It was there, at Haleiwa, that Henry found a hiding place in what was then a very remote corner of the world.

For years Henry lived and surfed alone in this paradise. He built a beach shack where he fished and surfed and had little contact with other surfers. Greg explains his first view of the waves of Haleiwa and of Henry.

*"One afternoon we were driving across the bridge at Haleiwa and I happened to notice that there was someone out in the water. I could see that he was Hawaiian and he was taking off on a neat little wave. We had never noticed any surf at Haleiwa, so we decided to try to find a way out there, to solve the mystery. We turned right at the Seaview Inn, on the road that heads out towards Kaena Point. We had never gone this way before. There were solid kiawe bushes between the road and the beach. No road leading in. The water was hardly visible except for that one spot off the bridge. We parked on the side of the road and cautiously made our way through the thorny kiawe, trying to find a path to the beach. Some farmers had their cows grazing there and we discovered one little cow path that led to the beach. We stepped out of the bushes and felt like we had emerged into Shangri-la. Here was a beautiful new surf spot and one lone Hawaiian, sitting out in the water on his surfboard, waving*

*to us to come join him, glad to have some company."*
—From *DA BULL, Life Over The Edge*

Noll paddled out, rode waves with Preece, and began a friendship that would last a lifetime. For years after that meeting, Greg's first stop in Hawaii was Henry's house. Haleiwa grew up around Henry, but Henry never left Haleiwa. He just stayed in that place and offered the fading spirit of Aloha to everyone he met.

Henry and Greg and their mutual friend, Buffalo, kept close contact over the years, but Greg lost touch with most of the other men with whom he had pioneered the North Shore. In February of 1993 Greg Noll held a big-wave rider's reunion at Makaha. Those attending the reunion included many of the big-wave riders from the old days: Tiger Espere, Peter Cole, Fred Hemmings, Fred Van Dyke, Kealoa Kaio, Billy Hamilton, Jock Sutherland, Rabbit Kekai, Ben Aipa, Buffalo Keaulana, Clyde Aikau, Bob Shepherd, and, of course, Henry Preece.

One evening the entire crew of legends were shuttled out to Waikiki from Makaha on a bus. Their final destination was *Duke's Canoe Club*, a classic restaurant in Waikiki where relics like Duke Kahanamoku's board are displayed. Rabbit Kekai talked of winning the Diamond Head Paddle Race on that board, and seeing Duke running to the water's edge to congratulate him afterwards.

After a night of eating, drinking, and music, Buffalo's wife, Momi, talked Greg into putting on a lava-lava in order to dance the hula. The legends hooted with perverse delight. The tourists in the crowd didn't know what to think. Then, like a little kid who had wet his pants in class, the legendary Greg Noll pleaded timidly, "Momi, why do you make me do these things?"

The party ended, the bus was loaded up, and everyone rolled back to Makaha. As we drove, most fell asleep, but I sat awake in the dark absorbing history and listening to the light hum of the road as a faint ukulele played somewhere near the front of the bus. Greg and Henry, who sat together in the back of the bus, talked and laughed and drank beer from Henry's cooler until Greg closed his eyes and leaned against the window. Henry faded next and leaned up against Greg. And there they sat, 40 years from their first meeting, dreaming of all of the waves they had ridden and the worlds they had discovered and conquered together. With their arms around each other's necks I heard Henry whisper lightly in beautiful pidgin English, "You know what brudah? When we die dey gonna put us in da same box." With that Henry leaned up against his old friend, closed his eyes and drifted with him out beyond time, into a world of endless waves. I thought I saw a tear fall from the eye of Greg Noll.

\*

# THE EFFORTLESS PRUNE

By the time that Chris O'Rourke had quit being afraid of the ocean he was 12 years old. That's when his older brother, Bart, who had already been surfing for two years, dragged him to La Jolla Shores and set him down next to his big surfboard in the wet sand near the water. Bart had hoped that Chris would become a good surfer, but little brother showed no promise of that whatsoever. He was a cry-baby, complaining about the cold water, and he was worried about being stung by a jellyfish. If Chris had his way, he would never enter the Pacific Ocean, but continue to comb the shore in his pursuit of sea shells.

Bart took a deep breath and tried to calm himself against the fidgeting boy. "Just try it once, you wimp," he said. "Just once and I'll leave you alone if you don't like it." The boy was unmoved by the attempted bribe, and didn't budge until Bart challenged him by saying, "You'd never be any good anyway." Looking at his little brother again, this time attempting to portray unfelt contempt, he shook his head and said, "You're no Skip Frye." Bart lifted the surfboard and prepared to leave for home. Chris glared at his brother angrily, wrenched the board from his arms, and with the victorious Bart close behind, entered the water. That was the extent of the instructions.

Bart pushed the kid out past the shorebreak, and shoved him toward the gentle, little waves where instinctively, awkwardly, the boy paddled toward the whitewater. Then he heard the voice of big brother, who was standing waist deep near the shore, screaming for him to turn around and catch the next whitewater wave. Hoping to finish with surfing and resume his search for shells, Chris cooperated by getting off the board, and clumsily kicking from the tail. This spun the board 180 degrees until the nose faced the shore. Then he laid flat on the board, paddled toward the beach, caught the whitewater and stood up with his arms over his head, looking toward his brother laughing and shouting "Skip Frye, Skip Frye," until the fin dragged on the sand and the boy fell down face first.

From then on Bart had trouble getting his board back. Chris O'Rourke had begun the long process of becoming a surfer, and it was all Bart's fault.

These were lean times in the O'Rourke home, and there was no money for surfboards. Determined to surf, nonetheless, Chris scoured the beaches near his home for Coke bottles, sold fruit stolen from the neighbor's trees, and then cut their lawns. Within two weeks he had saved the $25 necessary for a rotten foam and saltwater Gordon and Smith Surfboard. The board, which was covered with dust and cobwebs, had been stored in a garage, unridden for over five years. It had half a dozen unpatched dings, a cracked fin, and a faded picture of Jesus Christ resined onto the deck. It was too old to ride well and too new to be an antique. It was a worthless piece of junk which Chris took home and carefully sanded and polished with great care. He removed the dirty wax with hot water. Then he carved out the wax stuck into all the cracks and holes. He cut deeper into the foam, attempting riddance of the cancerous brown spots.

All that day and all the next day he mixed

batches of resin, sometimes putting in too much catalyst, and causing the mixture to catch fire. At other times he did not add enough catalyst. This left the resin wet in some places and brittle in others. Slowly, he filled the dings and patched the fin and sanded the resin down until the board was only slightly uglier than it had been two days ago.

It was early April then, and Chris and his friend, Tim Bessell, walked alone to La Jolla Shores from their homes near Windansea, two miles away. Neither one of them admitted to this, but they took that walk in order to avoid the heavy reef breaks, and find a beach with gentle sand instead of big rocks.

Once at the Shores, they raced each other into the lineup and then competed with each other in the surf, convinced in their minds that they were somehow ripping, unable to comprehend that they were not doing big, powerful turns, but merely tiny direction changes caused by trying to keep balance. Each felt superior as they watched the other lumber gracelessly along in a foul squat. Still they hooted for one another, and were good enough friends to ignore the other's blind remarks about their own ripping. On the beach, a group of local kids in their early teens stood around a blazing firering with shiny new boards and fashionable trunks. These kids were a little older than Chris and Tim. They were recognized as some of the best young surfers in La Jolla. Chris walked up and gave a friendly hello to the group, but when they eyed the plank, and the boy with the cut-off jeans, they turned away from him, talked lightly, and laughed loudly among themselves before glancing back at the new gremmie.

"Come on Chris, let's go get something to

eat" said Tim in hopes of avoiding confrontation. With that the pair laid their boards near the firering and walked the half mile to the market where they each bought a quart of chocolate milk and a dozen tiny sugar doughnuts.

On their way back to the beach they repeated familiar stories of their own rides, catching the big waves that nobody ever saw, and swearing on their mother's graves that each fantasy tube and cutback were as good as those done by Skip Frye. It was a hot, glassy afternoon and they broke into a run in order to get into the water quickly.

As they approached the beach, they could hear laughter. Then they smelled burning plastic, and noticed a black cloud forming on the horizon, spreading south with the wind. They saw the crew who had snubbed them earlier, standing around the firering, laughing and warming themselves on the black flames. Chris and Tim laughed too, thinking that someone had thrown a tourist's beach chair into the fire again. But when Chris saw what was fueling the fire he yelled out "My board! My board!" and ran over to save his beloved G & S from the flames. It was too late, however. The entire nose of the board had been destroyed, the stringer completely burned. Of the fiberglass, little remained but glowing red and black charcoal. He burned his hands retrieving the remains of the board from the flames.

The crew laughed hard as Chris put out the cinders of what had been his board in the damp sand. Then he turned to the group and yelled out, "Who did this?" Most of them looked embarrassed, and tried not to laugh while avoiding O'Rourke's penetrating eyes. "Who did this, who burned my board?" He shouted again. Then the biggest of the crew came forward. Puffing out his narrow chest to capacity, he smiled sarcastically, and said, "You call that a surfboard. I did you a favor kook." Chris lowered his head, clenched his fist, reached up above his head and tagged the big kid on the jaw as hard as he could, which was not very hard. There was no pain, and no blood from the weak punch, but the crew grabbed the aggressor and held him tightly within their many arms.

A little shaken, but still laughing at his attacker, the older boy said, "Split kook, you'd never be any good on that piece of shit anyway." Still restrained by the other kids, Chris shouted back, "Within a year I'll out surf you." He broke free and looked at each of them accusingly, and repeated, "I'll out surf all of you." They waited until he had gone a few feet before laughing nervously.

Gathering up what was left of his board, Chris walked back to the water's edge, looking over his shoulder periodically so that nobody could avoid his glare. Tim, who had also been restrained by the older kids, was now free, and walked up to comfort his friend. Tim turned away quietly when he noticed that Chris was crying. The tears embarrassed him, and he did not want them to embarrass Chris also. But the crying didn't last long, and Chris soon stood up, and began the long walk home with the ruined surfboard, picking up bottles as he went, holding each one like a first-place trophy before putting them into a paper sack.

Within a few days he had scrounged up enough money to buy surfboard patching materials from Mitch's Surf Shop. He cut out the dead foam, and then resined a new block of foam onto the nose which he shaped with file and sandpaper. He cut the cloth with his mother's scissors, and poured the resin from one of her aluminum pots. Mixing in purple pigment with the intention of hiding the flaws, the dark color further emphasized the unskilled labor. The result was that the nose of the board looked like a twisted and gnarled tree limb painted purple. It was worse than that really. The nose was thickly gobbed with resin, which never did completely harden in some areas, and hardened too quickly in other areas, leaving the purple mess cracked in places and permanently sand encrusted in others. The board, now uglier than ever, was christened by Chris' older sister, Lyn, "The Effortless Prune."

Each day after that, Chris walked to the Shores and surfed the Prune until dark, and then walked back home alone, sometimes past his enemies, who taunted him and mimicked the words "Within a year I'll out surf all of you." Chris never replied, however, he just kept walking, pretending not to notice. But now he had a new, unseen purpose. He intentionally let the words boil inside of him, in a deep place where they festered, and burned, and hardened into determination.

Chris' progress was rapid, even extraordinary. By mid-June he was riding well in the greenwater. By July he could turn and cutback. By August he was an average surfer. By September he was better than most of the kids his age.

Each year at the end of summer there was a surf contest for the kids at La Jolla Shores, and Chris found the two dollars to enter it in his sister's purse. For the weeks prior, he practiced longer and harder than ever, often surfing from dawn until dark. And each night he placed the board on his bed where he stood in his bare feet, visualizing turns and cutbacks, in order to get the feeling of surfing. Then he would sit in bed with the light on, going over and over the rules of the contest, and he would fall asleep clutching the contest rules and saying things like : "Do not stand up after the horn."

A light fog hung over the water in the pre-dawn hours as Chris paddled out alone with the rising sun. It was contest morning, and he would rehearse everything again for the last time. Here he faced the small and glassy surf, making sure that he had mastered every move he wanted to complete in competition. On the beach he read the rules again. As the day progressed, kids gathered on shore, some of them paddling out before the event began. Some were too confident for that, however, and just sat in the sand quietly waiting for their heats to start. All of the best gremmies in the area, and some from as far north as Redondo Beach had come to compete in this contest.

O'Rourke had an early heat, and he shook with cold and nerves as he put on his loose-fitting yellow jersey. Paddling out, he lost his board in the shorebreak before ever getting outside. He was embarrassed, certain that everyone was looking and laughing at him. He avoided looking to the beach, and swam hard for the board and retrieved it. Eventually anger and determination overcame nerves, and he caught two of the biggest set waves, and rode them without self-consciousness or excess, all the way to the sand. He caught three smaller waves also, falling only on his last one. Because of his extreme concentration on the event, he nearly stood up after the buzzer, something which would have disqualified him. He did not surf well then, but well enough to achieve third place in his first heat, which was barely enough to advance.

In his second heat, he had settled down a little and pulled off a good cover-up, almost a tube. He took second that time.

On his way to chocolate milk and doughnuts, he walked past the kid he had punched five months earlier. That kid had taken first in both of his heats, but most of his friends had been eliminated from the competition, and were involved in the ritual of complaining about their surfboards, the waves, or the judging. Chris looked directly at the tall kid, smiled, patted the Prune affectionately and walked on. Nobody laughed.

One of the judges noticed that O'Rourke was handicapped by his board, and offered him the use of one of his own boards, a perfectly crafted swallowtail, which Chris politely declined. The Prune and its rider were a part of each other, and stood out against the polish of the other boards and riders. It soon became the topic of conversation among the other surfers in the event, some of whom even attributed Chris' advancing to that board. The announcer, too, noticed Chris, and brought him up to the stand for a brief interview before the finals. "What's your strategy?" he asked.

"Just to do as good as I can, and get set waves," said Chris frankly. He didn't do as good as he could have, and he never did get any set waves. The tall kid had done that, and won the contest easily. Even if Chris had surfed his best, he was not as good as the tall kid. He held the trophy high, and gave Chris a nod of acknowledgment.

Chris walked home carrying his two most prized possessions, the Prune and his fifth-place ribbon. He intentionally took the long way as he headed for home, walking past the firering where some of the crew were lurking, admiring the big trophy that the tall kid had won. "You kicked that kook's ass, you kicked his ass," said somebody. O'Rourke, who happened to be walking by at the time, thrust his head toward the crew, motioned with his ribbon and said, " Hey, I've still got seven months to go."

✳

*Chris O'Rourke went on to become recognized as one of the best surfers in California, and one of the State's first professional surfers. He was never beaten by the tall kid again.*

# HOMECOMING

*Like all great surfers, Christopher Thomas O'Rourke was a fighter. He battled rocks and reefs and waves and anyone who stood between him and his longed-for victories. By the age of 14 he had beaten every competitive surfer in California. By 16 he had an even greater honor; Gerry Lopez had called him the best surfer he'd seen in the golden state. And now, only a year later, he lay in a hospital bed with a body broken by cancer and chemotherapy. Thinking that he had nothing left to fight with, the hospital staff pitied him. His friends and family, however, realized that he had only begun to fight.*

The surf had been good that day at Baja Malibu in Mexico, and O'Rourke was blasting out new territory with every wave. Then, suddenly he began feeling sick. He spun around and took off late, but unable to sense feeling in his hands, he jumped off his board. When he surfaced he noticed that half of his face was numb. He screamed for help, but had trouble forming words. Sensing a severe problem, O'Rourke's friends rescued him from the water and rushed across the boarder, to Scripps Hospital in La Jolla. Twenty-four hours later the surgeons had removed a massive brain tumor. The doses of chemotherapy increased in strength and frequency. He lost his hair, and was in such weakened condition that his doctors warned against any physical activity. "One bad fall could kill you," they said.

A strong Santa Ana wind had combined with a solid south swell on the day that I came by

Chris' house to interview him for the Australian surf magazine, *Tracks*. Only a few months had elapsed since the operation, and I was prepared for a depressing, morbid scene. Instead I found vigorous signs of life. Lying on the living room floor was a colorful, dripping wet surfboard. A red hockey helmet had been placed on top of it. I knew about the doctor's orders, and so could not put the athletic equipment together with O'Rourke. But there he was, sunburned, and happy, and wearing the white wicker hat that would become his trademark. The first words he spoke to me, "I went surfing today," sent an emotional chill through me, and I felt that I had connected with his primary passion.

Chris described the six-foot surf at Windansea, going into detail about every good wave he had ridden. "On one wave I pulled this snap right beneath the lip, and drove off the bottom, and into 'Right Hooker,' (the hollow inside section at Windansea)." His hands carved long arcs in the air as he spoke, and, having seen him surf in his prime, I was able to imagine the rides he described. He pulled off his hat and gently placed my hand over soft, pulsating skin. There was a soft spot the size of a grapefruit where his skull had been removed after brain surgery. "That's where they did the operation. Eventually, when the swelling goes down, they're going to give me a plate. Then I won't have to worry about getting hurt. Until then, I can use this," he said smiling broadly holding up the hockey helmet.

He continued to surf with the helmet on, and even managed third place in a pro contest, behind two of the top surfers in the world at the time, Larry Bertelman and Rory Russell. And he continued to retain his position at Windansea as the best surfer in that break. He was only 19 years old, and he had plans to recover, and join the newly formed international pro surfing tour. Noting his ability and determination, this goal did not seem impossible.

Within less than a year the plate was put into his head. He surfed hard, sometimes recklessly, ignoring doctor's advice that he take it easy. His hot temper seemed the biggest obstacle to a long life, however, and he would often explode in anger if he felt threatened or mistreated. A kid had sent a hamburger patty out to him raw. "You cooked it, you're going to eat it," said O'Rourke before throwing the raw meat in the cook's face.

O'Rourke was going to Australia as coach for the American team. At the airport, he emptied his pockets of keys and other metallic objects. He walked through the metal detector, and the alarm went off. He removed his watch, and it rang again. Again he walked through, and again the alarm sounded. Finally, he removed his hat, pointed to the scar covering the new plate in his head, and shouted to the security guard, "Okay, you win, I've got a bomb planted in there!" After being searched by security, he was eventually allowed to board the plane.

In Australia, O'Rourke began feeling weak and sick, something that he passed off as jet lag. One morning he awoke early, but fell to the floor after trying to walk. Put on an emergency flight by Hawaiian judge Jack Shipley, O'Rourke was rushed back to the States where he was hospitalized and put through many painful tests until it was determined that a tumor was growing around his spinal cord. This was the final burden.

Nobody had ever managed to walk after

this particular type of surgery had been performed upon them. He was unable to walk, but he somehow figured that he would be able to surf. Knowing that this sounded ridiculous, he kept his surfing plans secret, conning a friend to drive him to the beach and lay him onto his board in the calm inside water. The friend pulled Chris from his wheelchair, and laid him in the shallow water. Then, before the friend could react, Chris had paddled away and out into the break. There, amid cries of protest, O'Rourke turned the board around, and took off on a set wave. He slid to the bottom in perfect position, pushed up with his arms and tried to stand. But he was betrayed by his paralyzed legs. The wave looped over him and rolled him mercilessly in the shorebreak where he was retrieved by the friend.

Rehabilitation was slow. It took months, but Chris made medical history by moving with a walker, then a cane. Then he abandoned the cane, and bought a skateboard. Three friends stood above Windansea in the early morning chill, on the steep slope of Nautilus Street. One of the friends held O'Rourke on a skateboard. At Chris' request, he let him go. Then he rode unsteadily down hill for about 20 feet. He did one little turn before he landed in the arms of another friend who stood down the street. Then the first friend walked down the street and waited until Chris was dropped to him. Thus, the three friends made their way down the street, all the way to the surf of Windansea where Chris was forced to stop and look at the surf. He walked with great pain and effort to the water's edge. It was small and glassy, and he just looked at the waves without saying anything.

For weeks Chris worked with his friends

on his skateboarding until he was able to ride the board by himself. Within a short time he was doing turns and cutbacks, and becoming a good skateboarder again. I arrived at his house one weekend and found that Chris had his surfboard waxed and ready. He asked me to drive him to La Jolla Shores. There he paddled out and rode four or five small waves, not with his usual flair, but well enough to enjoy himself immensely.

The next day we went to Swami's where O'Rourke met up with Brad Gerlach, the hot new gremmie who would, in ten years, finish second on the ASP Tour. Chris held onto Brad's leg and was paddled back out to the inside section after each successive wave. Chris surfed small waves whenever he could for the next six months.

One day Windansea was breaking a solid six feet, and O'Rourke looked out from the parking lot to see his friend, Tim Seniff, getting a good ride all the way through to the inside. Somebody commented on Senniff's ability, saying that Tim was the best surfer in the water. While O'Rourke appreciated his friend's ability, he was intolerant of being considered second-best at "his" break Chris grabbed his board and paddled out.

The aggressive pack in the water were surprised. Some of them had heard that Chris was dead. Others, who had seen him months earlier, were convinced that he would never surf again. Nobody expected to see him out at Windansea during a swell. And nobody dropped in on him. His friends greeted him with guarded optimism, and ran interference for him, keeping him protected from the anonymous pack who just whispered among themselves, and looked over at him, remembering that he had once dominated this spot.

Chris saw the wave he wanted, a six-foot peak that popped up and stretched down the beach in an uneven line. The inside section looked, to the untrained eye, like a closeout. O'Rourke dropped in, did a stiff bottom turn, and pushed his board up into the lip where he hung high before pushing down on his inside rail. He coasted slowly to the bottom and gained speed. He was feeling alive again as he loosened up and outran each section. He did another turn, better this time.

He was moving fast when he hit Right Hooker, his favorite section. There, animal instinct took over. He put his arm into the wave in order to slow down, and folded himself into a tiny ball, allowing the tube to pour over him as he became invisible from the beach. By now everyone on the beach was on their feet, yelling wildly with their arms in the air.

It was not a long tube, but he was certainly in it, and he came flying out over the top, and stood tall before looking defiantly back at Sennif, falling and screaming, "I'm back!" The beach crowd went wild.

Someone in Levis and a T-shirt paddled the board back out. "Thank God I can surf. I can surf," O'Rourke said, lifting his arms into the air.

Later the paddler described O'Rourke's eyes as bright blue and shining, saying that he was smiling and tingling with goose bumps from cold and adrenaline.

That was the last wave that Chris O'Rourke ever rode. Like every wave of his entire life, he rode it with all his heart.

★

# THE PHANTOM

*The following is a story that I have heard for more than 30 years.*

When Phil Edwards was a kid he used to surf an out of the way spot in Carlsbad called Guayule, named after the artificial rubber processing plant located near by. Because Phil surfed there so frequently, and so well, he became known as "The Guayule Kid."

Occasionally, the surfers from Windansea would travel north to Guayule, and bring their champion, Bobby Patterson. The Windansea group insisted that Bobby was the best, while those from up north argued that Phil was better. Since there were few contests, the controversy was never officially settled.

And since there was no media, few outside of his area knew what Phil Edwards looked like. Phil didn't care, he just surfed in relative obscurity for hours each day, until he was, as Dale Velzy puts it, "just shining."

As the story goes, Phil would drive north to Malibu where the crowds were hostile to outsiders. There Phil would grab an umbrella and move awkwardly by intention, through the sand, dragging his balsa board in his free arm. By the time he reached the water's edge, he had been ordered off the beach half a dozen times. Undaunted, he paddled out, kicking his board from the tail, and falling off periodically.

Once in the lineup, he'd allow himself to drift back to the north of the point until he was further back than anyone had ever been before. All eyes were on him as he paddled for the biggest wave of the set. There were already giggles coming from the pit crew, who knew what was going to happen next—the kook would paddle and eat it while his board rode alone into the rocks. Well, it didn't happen quite that way. The kook took off as planned, but after that everything was different—everything, including the way that people rode waves at Malibu. Phil planted an edge and ran up into trim, which caused him to move really fast. Then he ran up further to the nose, nearly hanging five, and trimming across the wall where he sped past the surfers standing like statues on the inside. Now, moving out at full speed, he raced the wave in the hook all the way to the sand. Those in the water and on the beach were stunned. Nobody had ever ridden a wave from that far back before.

Before anyone could get the phantom's name, he was riding down Coast Highway in his car with a satisfied smile on his face.

For 30 years I had been curious, and finally, last year, I had the opportunity to ask Phil Edwards if this was a true story. He just laughed, shook his head and said emphatically, "I would never do a thing like that!"

★

# A GREMMIE REMEMBERS MISTER PIPELINE

*People were scattering, reverently clearing the sidewalks of Avenida de La Revolucion in Tijuana as if a priest, or a cop were coming through. I was forced into the gutter by the parting crowd, and looked up, above the mass, to see the top of a black felt hat, it's crown bobbing steadily, smoothly, up and down, and moving forward. When the wearer of the hat came into view I recognized him immediately, and I, along with most everyone else in the street, watched him pass. He smiled as if giving his blessing, yet transmitting with his eyes an undercurrent of danger. The cool, purposeful movement of a gunfighter at high noon said that he had earned the cleared sidewalk. I watched him slink down the uneven concrete and then hook into a dark bar. That was the only time that I ever saw him in person.*

 *Of course I had heard of him — every surfer had. We gremmies worshiped him, or, more accurately, the images of him taken from magazines and surf movies of his impossible rides on that red board at Pipeline, smiling big when he made it, and bigger when he did not. "Black Butch," and "Mister Pipeline" were the names awarded by those who admired his bad power. He referred to himself as "The Old Dutchman." But when I filled out my Surfer Poll ballot that year, I simply wrote the name Butch Van Artsdalen in the number-one spot.*

 *From what I had seen in films and magazines he was the best. What I couldn't learn from the surf media, I filled in with the stories I heard from the older guys.*

 *One of them told me that Butch was afraid*

*to go home because he had 11 girlfriends. Eleven girlfriends! Then there was the story of how he hated wearing shoes for any reason. When the airlines demanded he wear shoes in order to board the plane for Hawaii, he decided instead to camouflage himself in a black suit and tie, but with no shoes. They let him on the plane.*

*Another time I heard that he had beaten up the toughest man in all of Mexico in a street brawl. They tore through three streets, the fight lasting for over an hour, until both men were exhausted. Finally Butch landed one hard punch that downed his foe. He stood, swaying unsteadily over the man while keeping his fists cocked. The other man lay still, as if dead, in a bloody heap.*

*By all accounts Butch liked nothing more than to surf and to party with his friends. And he didn't mind a fair fight if someone was trying to steal his good time. A fearless surfer, a partier, a brawler when necessary—I've found that an accurate, but narrow view of him.*

*Fifteen year-old Hank Warner, a sunburned and stoked gremmie from Pacific Beach who actually held the generic name "Gremmie," saw Butch differently, from the ground up. In a town filled with legendary surfers, Butch was Gremmie's number-one hero.*

*But the first time that Gremmie saw Butch, he didn't like him. Here was a man with massive square shoulders winning a paddling race around the Pacific Beach Pier, and leaving the second-best paddlers of the day (many of whom were like big brothers to the kid) far behind. And the way he surfed, winning every contest without really trying, made the legends look bad by comparison.*

*But Butch soon won Gremmie's friendship through his phenomenal surfing and many acts of kindness. He helped the kid with his paper route, gave him tips on handling big surf, and made it known that he would be there for him if any inland thugs tried to start anything.*

*Hank's admiration grew when he saw the great rides at Butch's pre-Pipeline training ground, a vicious reef considered unrideable by most in those days, Big Rock. At Windansea, Butch was king, often whirling around into helicopters five years before anyone else even thought them possible. Once he rode a board with one fin on the nose and one on the tail, spinning around, making the nose the tail and the tail the nose all the way to the beach. He could do anything he liked on a wave, but mostly he just rode deep and hard in the meanest tubes he could find.*

*Gremmie had seen all of the big men who came looking for Butch and went home broken and bloody. The big days when nobody but Butch would paddle out. The trophies held modestly low at the contests. In time, Butch's victories became Gremmie's victories also, and a pride from being a friend of the Dutchman's began to grow in him. He remembered it all, and in later years would pull out the stories as if they were photos mounted in a scrapbook. One his favorite recollections concerns a trip taken with Butch to San Miguel, Mexico.*

The surf was a solid four to five feet, and mirror glassy all day, peeling from the rocky point to the jetty as Hank and Butch traded waves in the solitary blue water. Then, after losing his board, and picking his way to the beach over the sharp rocks, Gremmie's feet were pierced by countless sea urchin spines. He pulled his board to the sand, limped onto the jetty, and sat there feeling so happy that he hardly noticed the purple needles which he pulled from his slightly bleeding heels.

Butch had taught the gremmie not to cower from pain. Hank watched Butch fade, make a sweeping power turn, run to the nose and pull into the tube. On the next wave he sat in the barrel until he came out switch-stance. Here was a magic beyond words, a certain something almost supernatural that only the best surfers in the world had—an unreasonable way with the ocean. He should have fallen when the lip hit him in the head, but he rolled with the power, worked with it if he could, against it if he had to. He surfed hard, and overcame each wave, getting spectacular rides that nobody but Hank would ever see.

Wave after wave, he came from too far back, deep in the pocket with a beautiful defiance and an economy of movement. After one deep barrel the gremmie said aloud, to nobody, "He's the best in the world." As if to prove that point Butch stuffed all ten feet of his board into a five foot pocket on the next wave. He disappeared for long seconds, racing behind the curtain before he was knocked down by a little inside section. The red board came floating in. Butch bodysurfed on the next wave, chasing the board like a fish chases a lure. As he came to shore, he smiled the way he always did when he wiped out, or rode in the tube.

The tube. That's where Butch Van Artsdalen seemed most comfortable, the perfect hiding place for someone who did not want to conform to a mechanical society in shoes.

As he picked his way over the rocks toward him, Hank recalled the night a few years earlier when Bud Brown's surf movie *Gun Ho* came to Mission Bay High School. It was there, on the big screen, driving out of big, dangerous barrels, and smiling—once casually sitting down and dusting off his hands in deep satisfaction for a job well done, that Gremmie finally understood the extent of Butch's power. The gremmie had shouted louder than anyone that night, and waited in reverence for just a moment before jumping on the backs of the others who dog-piled Butch in honor of his miracle.

Every day for two years he had looked up at the *Surfer Magazine* centerfold of Butch at Pipeline taped above the refrigerator. He would sometimes crouch on his bed to imitate the stance, once in a while sitting down and dusting off his hands to make the dream seem more real. And now he was here, alone, in perfect waves with the best surfer in the world.

The sky had deepened to dark blue and a few stars had already come out when Butch started up the cherry-red '57 Ford Station Wagon, and told Hank to get in. They went to Ensenada for dinner and a few beers.

Dinner was there as promised, but the few beers became many beers, coming fast and sometimes chased by tequila or other evil drinks at Hussong's Cantina until Butch was reduced to a happy lump on a barstool.

The gremmie had ordered a beer too, but he sipped it cautiously and with displeasure, pouring most of it into the red clay flower pot when nobody was looking. When he was finished, he rocked back in his chair and then came forward where he pounded the bottle on the bar just like he had seen John Wayne do in the movies. The gesture was wasted, however. Butch was too drunk to notice.

A few hours later Butch cleared a mountain of glass from the table with his big right arm, stood up, paid his bill, and threw his keys to the kid, shouting, "Gremmie, get us out of here." The keys rattled in Hank's hand as he walked out the door and told Butch that he was too young to drive. But Butch rested a big hand on Hank's shoulder, looked down to where he stood, smiled and said firmly, "Just get us home, Gremmie. Just get us home."

Gremmie walked and Butch stumbled to the car, steadying himself on the sides of the wooden building, or on Hank, or on anything else upright and stable. Mister Pipeline opened the car door, sat down hard in the passenger seat, rolled his window down and bid *adios* to his friends at the bar. In the car, he fell asleep immediately, smiling.

Hank looked over at his hero with some sadness. He knew that Butch sometimes drank too much, and it bothered him. But beyond that was the fearful knowledge that the life of a great surfer, the greatest surfer, rested solely in the unsure hands of a gremmie. A gremmie was someone you tied to the pier and christened with R. C. Cola. Someone who bragged loudly of riding huge waves but was nowhere to be seen when the big north swells came. A gremmie could not be trusted with such an important task as this.

Maybe he could leave the car there and have someone else drive them home. He looked around—there was no one else. It was up to him now, and he knew that he would need Pipeline courage to make it.

As Hank sat in the driver's seat, his eyes

hit level with the dashboard of the car. He took some comfort in noticing that it did not look much different than that of his mother's "Country Squire," the one she had allowed him to start up once and back out of the driveway for her. That driving lesson ended abruptly, however, when Hank mowed down the flowerbed and creamed the wooden fence.

Hank closed his eyes, turned the key of the Red Hornet, which is what Butch called his station wagon, and it roared to life. The power scared the kid, and everything in him wanted to turn off the engine. Instead he forced himself to grab a handful of wadded up T-shirts from the back seat. After he placed them beneath himself, he was able to see over the dashboard. Barely. He piled up more laundry beneath himself until he was looking over the wheel and into the dimly lit street ahead.

Cautiously he let off the emergency brake. Then he moved the stick to "D" and pushed down on the throttle which caused the Hornet to lunge forward abruptly. In a panic, he slammed on the brakes. The car stalled. Butch just sat there, asleep and smiling. Fearfully Hank tried again, repeating the process, but making sure this time to touch the gas pedal lightly, and to turn the wheel gently. The car slid away from the curb and down the road, hitting every pothole dead on, but never waking Butch.

Gremmie moved through the nearly deserted streets, picking his way back to the main highway before he realized that his lights were off, and that he had seen Hussong's Cantina twice since leaving the curb. "I've been driving in circles!" he said aloud, hoping to alert Butch so that he would drive home. But Butch was frozen in place, snoring now, and with that same satisfied smile on his face. Hank smacked into a high curb, and turned off the car as he sat there shaking, nearly too frightened to try driving again.

It was dark now and all of the cantinas had closed. There were no taxis nearby. There was nothing to do but start the car and try again.

He put the stick in "R," backed up, shifted into "D," and started down the road again. He rolled through town, one time crossing over into on-coming traffic, twice nearly running down pedestrians, one who swore at him in one of the few Spanish words that he understood. He bounced up onto the sidewalk, and rode on it for about 25 feet before coming down hard on the street again. And Butch just sat there asleep and smiling.

The gremmie was a talented, precocious kid, and in little time he got the hang of driving, weaving through the city cautiously. His fear decreased greatly when he finally saw the blackness of the edge of town and the road back to San Miguel.

Except for the big trucks which came too close and sent the car swaying, the long straight-away was an easy drive. Gremmie rolled down his window and rested his arm on the cold metal, thinking the entire time, "I can drive now. I can drive."

And so the gremmie drove along the dark road, past shadows of skinny cows and brown smoking hills on one side, and empty black water sometimes lined in whitewater on the other side. He turned his head and looked toward the ocean as he had seen Butch do on their way into town. By doing this he did not so much hope to discover a trace of swell, but to trick himself into believing that he was completely relaxed behind the wheel. Another trick he played on himself was to turn the radio up and sing along with the soul music of *XERB*. He laid back in the seat with fake confidence and authentic pride. Looking over, he saw Butch unmoved, smiling, crammed warmly into the corner, apparently dreaming something good.

"That's Butch Van Artsdalen; I'm driving Butch Van Arts-da-len home in his car" he said softly as he giggled to himself and slapped the wheel with one hand. Hank's confidence and joy increased for real as he drove. Once he even made a big "S" turn, pretending to surf on the road. The move made him laugh nervously. But even that did not stir his passenger.

The few lights in the distance indicated the little village of San Miguel. And while he felt mostly relief, he was also a little sorry that the rescue would come to an end so abruptly. Still, he would make the left turn into the dusty lot, and drive down to the campsite where Butch would wake, take a long piss on the dirt, thank him for driving, and crawl into the canvas tent with all of his clothes on.

The gremmie's new confidence also brought on other visions. He would ride deep in the tube tomorrow, just as deep as Butch had ridden today. And he would turn hard under the lip, and run to the nose at the last second. He would...."STOP THE CAR. STOP. STOP THE CAR!" The words hit him like a punch, and brought him back to the dark road where he shivered, clutching the wheel tightly in fear until he realized that it was the voice of Butch, now fully awake, sitting up electrically, screaming, and patting his tangled hair as if hoping to find the hat that was not there on the top of his head.

In a reactionary flash Hank stomped on the brakes causing a loud screech of rubber. The entire contents of the car came hurling forward as blankets, towels, pants, and T-shirts pinned them up against the windshield.

After the recoil Butch cleared the mess around himself quickly, and glared at Hank, who was still digging himself out of the Levi and T-shirt mountain. When the car had come to a complete stop, Butch sat up straight, resumed patting his messed up hair, and shouted, "My hat! Where's my hat? Go back. Go on, go back." There was no question about it; they were going back.

The gremmie's entire victory collapsed around him as he swung the car in a wide U turn, and nearly drove off of the steep shoulder. He knew that this was a hopeless quest, for Mexico had a way of claiming things and never giving them up again. Only today he had lost a sleeping bag in broad daylight. How could they find a hat in the dark?

But he drove back to Ensenada while Butch hung out the window looking on the black road, in the black air, for a black hat. Hank feared that Butch would lead them back to town, to the cantina, and to jail for driving without a license. The idea of a Mexican jail made little tears well up in Hank's eyes. The vision was a bad one now, and then, "Stop the car. Stop. Stop the car!"

Being more prepared this time, Hank managed a little bit less jerky stop, and pulled over to the shoulder of the road. Here Butch got out of the car, and then crawled on the edge of the road, searching for a hat that was not there. Hank just sat behind the wheel with tears in his eyes, thinking of home. Then, piercing the darkness, Hank heard a laugh, and a large, booming voice jubilantly announcing, "Got it. I got it." He looked up to see Butch swaying in the headlights, holding the hat tightly in both hands, laughing and shouting victoriously.

Butch was soon back in the passenger seat wearing the dusty black hat squarely on his head. He went back to sleep wearing that same happy smile as before.

Hank made another wide U turn which pointed them back to San Miguel, and soon the sparse lights of the trailers in the village were visible again. And again the fantasies crept up and around Hank, and possessed him until he saw himself at Pipeline, second in command, riding big, deep barrels on the screen while his friends hooted in disbelief, giving him the same dog-pile celebration that they had previously been reserved only for Butch. Like Butch he would be a humble, friendly star. He would help young gremmies get their start. And the world would know how the two of them conquered Banzai Pipeline. They would have a nice house on the beach, right at Pipeline and... "Stop. Stop the Car!"

In spite of the abrupt command, Hank came to a relatively smooth stop this time, and looked to see Butch, now with his hat in his hands, tracing an index finger around its base. His eyes were huge with worry. "My hatband. My hatband. Where's my hatband?" he shouted with an intensity that insisted that anyone in range share his concern. Hank knew that they would not get safely home until Butch found that hatband. After all, it had been made as the twin of the collar worn by "Lucky," Butch's black labrador. Like all things that depended upon him, Butch was deeply sentimental about that dog. Hank spun the car around again, this time with a precision gained by much practice, and began another lap, back toward Ensenada. Then Butch, with his blurry, drunk, but athletic eyes, somehow spotted the thin black strip of engraved leather on the side of the road. Hank stopped the car upon command, perfectly this time, and Butch walked out with the dignity of an intoxicated butler, grabbed the leather strip, and held it high like a trophy before putting it onto the hat which he mashed onto his head.

Once again he lay down to sleep with a broad smile. This time, however, he did not move, and Hank drove cautiously home and into the San Miguel parking lot.

The next morning the waves were good at San Miguel, but there was nobody out to ride them. Except for the changed expression on his face, which had gone from smiling to agape and unsmiling, nothing was different for Mister Pipeline. He sat still in the passenger seat, fast asleep, covered by the blanket that Gremmie had put around him. His black hat, a little dented, sat squarely on his head, with the hat-band firmly around it.

Gremmie too was sound asleep, sprawled out all over the tent as if he owned it. He was smiling, dreaming of conquering Pipeline.

*

*At a memorial service for Butch Van Artsdalen in La Jolla, the words of Billy Caster were the only ones that could comfort Hank Warner. "There never could have been a 40-year-old Butch Van Artsdalen," said Caster. Mister Pipeline died in Hawaii on July 17, 1979. He was 39 years old.*

# THE ARK

A streak of golden light moved just above the heat waves of the black road like a 2,000 pound, extraterrestrial canary. Blasting its way through the eucalyptus forest, the streak turned and twisted and mashed its way toward me before slowing down and coasting over the gravel shoulder where I stood hitchhiking from Noosa Heads to Byron Bay. Then I could see that it was nothing more than a 1966 Dodge Dart. The Dart's operator pulled up next to me, rolled down the window and stared blankly in my direction, his cement-blond pompadour pointing like a good hunting dog.

I sought instruction from him, but he sat as still as a porcelain Elvis. When I asked him where he was going, he silently motioned down the road with his big, hard hair. Assuming that he was offering me a ride, I loaded my board into his car, threw my pack into the back seat, and climbed aboard. He took off like a shot, checked his watch and said aloud, to himself, "One hundred kilometers in one hour." Then he tromped down forcefully and bent the laws of physics all the way to the Gold Coast. Through the city of Brisbane he skidded and swerved and scared the crap out of me, rarely slowing down, never muttering a word to me, but driving with dedication to some unspoken cause, which seemed somehow related to time. He checked his watch again and said, "100 kilometers in one hour."

Relieved by the sight of good surf, I asked him to drop me off at Kirra. There I thanked him for the ride, and he addressed me for the first time. Flicking his sunglasses up until they rested on his forehead, he smiled, extended his hand for shaking and said, "If you ever get to Mullumbibi, you tell 'em you met the Dart." He peeled down the highway and was gone, beyond sight, when I looked again a moment later.

Kirra was good, four foot and fun, and Michael Peterson was out, moving his metronome arm to hold a tempo that nobody else could keep. I surfed for two hours, and came in only because it was getting dark. It started to rain before I even dried off, and I wanted to make Byron Bay by nightfall. Again I hitched, counting myself lucky to be picked up by three people in a recreational vehicle.

The driver, a soft-spoken, middle-aged man, introduced himself as Colin. A middle-aged woman, whom I figured for his wife, was named Sheila. The teenaged girl, whom I figured as their daughter, was named Janet. I was wrong about them. I soon learned that they were unrelated, and had met only weeks earlier when they escaped together from a mental institution, stolen the RV we were driving in, and had been cruising the coast in search of good, twisted fun.

We drove through Byron Bay and Colin pulled in, just south of town, into the Broken Head caravan park as the rain hit hard. After settling on a level spot, Colin walked outside without excusing himself, Sheila and Janet retreated to the back of the RV and returned quickly, giggling, wearing nothing but silk panties. Janet sat near me, almost on my lap. Apparently referring to Colin she said, "He's bonkers mate."

Sheila nodded in agreement, hung her crying head and said, "He's so violent; sometimes it scares me." Stunned, I had no reply. I stared out a window, wondering if the weather would allow me to sleep outside, away from all of them.

Suddenly Colin threw the door open, and stood tall before us, cradling a .22 caliber rifle. He looked at Sheila and Janet, who were pulling away from him in fear, covering themselves with their hands, and clutching onto the tablecloth in an attempt to hide their nakedness. "Mongrel," screamed Colin at me. I give you shelter, and this is the thanks I get! You want my women, well go ahead, take them!" He grabbed Janet roughly and threw her at me. I shut my eyes to pray silently. The steel of the rifle was cold against my temple and I was frozen at the dinner table. Then — *click* — and loud laughter as the women poured themselves around Colin, holding and kissing him passionately.

"Your luck's changed, Mate," said Colin, pushing Sheila toward me as if she were an offering from him. I pushed her aside, grabbed my pack and my board and ran from the caravan through the deep mud, listening to their fading laughter as I sloshed about, trying to put distance between myself and my captors.

Sheets of rain fell from a black sky as I stumbled frantically, hoping that I was free from them. I continued to tromp through the mud, but was often unable to grip the earth, and fell repeatedly as I moved in a wet and dirty daze. Unfamiliar with the area, I wandered for an hour or so, until, with no other place to go, I walked to the door of the first habitat I saw, a rundown wooden house, with a large water tank adjacent to it.

A bearded man answered the door, and compassionately, gently, invited me inside.

"Have you had any tucker, Mate?" He asked as I stood, covered in mud on the warm, dirt floor. Before I could reply, he had my coat hung up on a wooden peg. He excused himself for a moment and then returned with a pair of overalls, which I changed into in the bathroom. Then he took me to a big, square room with a wooden picnic table in the midst of it. There sat two young men, both with long hair and beards, eating from bowls, without looking up, like wild dogs. They moved aside and I sat down beside them to salad, fish, and red wine poured into a broken fruit jar.

The bearded man was named Dave. He introduced me to Brian, and Bill, who once they had eaten, turned out to be equally as polite and gentle as Dave. They were all three Australian surfers, drawn from Sydney to Byron Bay because of its warm climate and good surf.

They never asked me about myself, but fell into a conversation, which I found was perpetual among them, about surfing, their vegetable garden, and women, which because of their isolation, none of them had been near in six months. After a lively game of cards and some more wine, I was shown to a corner of the frontroom and given a blanket and a bedroll. I slept peacefully while the light rain kept rhythm for my dreams on the tin roof.

The day was sudden and beautifully blue as I looked out of a window onto rolling, green hills. Dave wandered in and put a cup of hot tea into my hands which I took gratefully. Crouching near my bed, he looked around at the old wooden structure, planted a hand on a beam, breathed deeply and said affectionately, "Ah, the Ark." He stood, and paced, looking reverently at the tall beams as he continued. "This place was an abandoned barn when Dave, Brian and I found it and turned it into our home." Then he paused before turning to me with a stern admonishment, "You've got to keep the doors closed when you're away or one of the older goats in the neighborhood will try to wander in. They still think its their home, poor bastards."

Dave was warmed up and comfortable now, and speaking like a friendly tour guide. "We call it the Ark because it survived last year's flood when water on the road was as high as a horses mane," he said, holding his arm level with his chest to show me just how high that was. He continued to look lovingly at the old barn for a moment and then he stopped as if he had forgotten what he had originally come to say, "Breakfast is ready if you want any."

I found my way outside where oatmeal steamed in a large metal pot beside a pitcher of fresh, cold milk and wild berries. We ate on a wooden bench beneath a sky that shone so brightly blue that you could not look upon it for too long. Drops of water occasionally spilled from the leaves of one of the many eucalyptus trees, and rippled the surface of someone's oatmeal. Quiet conversation and the songs of many loud parrots, who crowded near the table for the scraps that we did not have, were the only sounds.

A few hundred yards down a dirt track, one of Australia's most beautiful beaches produced long, fast waves, peeling around a headland. "It'll be good today," said Dave unhurriedly while glancing casually at the ocean. The surf was good that day. And the next day, and for many days in a row after that.

Nobody ever offered it, but after a week it

seemed that I had been accepted as a tenant of the Ark. I was very happy there until one morning when Dave approached me saying, "We've got a problem mate."

"They're going to ask me to leave," I thought, trying to hide my sadness, and wondering where I would go next.

"Mate," Dave repeated, putting a big, gentle hand on my shoulder, "we're two months behind on the rent, and we're going to be given the boot." I had less than $100 to my name, but asked my gracious host if there was anything that I could do to help out.

"No mate, the rent's two bucks a week, plus a dollar a month for utes. That means we owe the old man..." He paused to count on his fingers. Then he raised his wooly head and said, "Eighteen bucks!"

I turned and walked over to my backpack, giggling to myself at the tiny sum, before pulling out $20.00, which I turned over to Dave. Not a man used to such miracles, he did nothing but stare at the bill at first. Then he felt it with his fingers as if to make sure it was real. Finally he laughed loudly, and held the bill between his thumbs and forefingers as he danced a sort of jig, while screaming out "We're saved! We're saved!" The boys gathered round to see the miracle and touch the 20 before they took turns hugging me warmly as Dave continued to dance and shout.

The next day, after surfing all morning, Brian was asked to go into town and pay the rent. He had only gone a fraction of the ten kilometers, when Officer Shales, the town cop, observed Brian's long hair swaying in the breeze and pulled over next to him. Shales offered Brian a ride just as he always did, and Brian happily jumped into the front seat, knowing that the cost of the ride was a speech. "Now, Brian, you know that I don't like hippies much, but you and yer mates seem okay to me. If you were a good bloke, you'd cut your hair and get a job." Brian, who liked everybody he ever met and desperately wanted Shales to think of him as a good bloke, said that he would cut his hair that day if it would make Officer Shales feel any better. Then he offered to shout the officer a beer at the pub, once he was off duty.

That evening Shales poured Brian from the squad car, and Brian happily bumped his way toward the Ark. Shales honked at the door and waved to us, as Brian, who was now shorn of beard, and wearing a flat-top, just like the one that Officer Shales had, stumbled up the drive and into the house. We helped him to the kitchen, placing the wrinkled receipt hanging out of his shirt pocket, and the opened gallon of wine in his hand, on the table.

Food was never a problem at the Ark; the boys grew it or fished for it. Wine, on the other hand, was not something that they saw every day, although they would have liked to. I was a bit discouraged when I read the receipt: "Paid: $13.00 for back rent. The remainder owed one week from today."

Bill and Dave took turns drinking from the bottle while I tried to address the rent problem. They were all very polite not to interrupt me. When I finished my talk, Dave said that I had a gift for public speaking, and should consider doing it for a living. The others agreed that it was a good speech, and lifted their fruit jars to me. But they were too happy to talk about the rent now. They were warm and fed and they had a bottle of wine to drink.

The next morning, Brian was up early, combing and waxing the new flat-top. He liked the new look, but seemed upset by something. "I promised Officer Shales that I would get a job," said Brian, when asked why he was unhappy.

"Don't do it, said Bill. You never keep your promises, you been promising to do the dishes for over a year, and they never have been done by you, have they!"

Brian sat and thought for a moment, with the silent recognition that Bill was right about the dishes. "This is different mate. Yesterday Officer Shales and I became friends, and after I got me haircut, he said he was proud of me, and with a tear in his eye, he said that I was like a son to him."

The boys knew this was serious, but they had no idea of how to solve Brian's problem. Brian was intelligent and handy, but he hadn't had a steady job for ten years, not since he was 12 years old and got fired from his paper route for spending all of the money he received on candy and Christmas presents for his little brothers. There were few jobs around Byron Bay, but as a formality we ran them by Brian one at a time. "What about the pub, as a barman? " offered Bill.

"No, said Dave, he'd always be giving piss away, and he'd get fired."

"What about on the fishing boats?" said Dave, who answered himself by saying that Brian was too kind-hearted to kill fish.

Brian sat with his head in his hands as one by one, every job in town was eliminated for him. Within a week Brian had nearly forgotten about employment. It was time to pay the rent, however, and so I once again gave him a 20.

Again, he paid part of it, putting the rest into a bottle. After two months of employing Brian's method, I was as broke as he was. Within another month there was another eviction notice.

For the entire time that I lived in the Ark, I had not known anyone there to have a job. One night Dave called a meeting. The boys looked sad, the way they did when the surf went flat. "Mates, we've got a problem," began Dave. One of us is going to have to go in Friday and work Cooper's flower fields." Bill ducked his head shyly. Brian sat, eyes wide, looking stunned and horrified, while remembering his promise to Shales. "I'll go," he said sourly, volunteering to sacrifice himself for his friends.

"No," said Dave to Brian abruptly. When we have an emergency, we do things the democratic way. Dave held out four straws in his hand. After we had all picked, he put his head down in defeat. His straw was the short one. Feeling that Dave was troubled, I offered to accompany him to work the next day. Brian went along out of a sense of duty to Shales, and Bill went along out of a sense of duty to all of us.

We worked, picking flowers for eight hours. At the end of the day we received cash for our labor, and went to the pub, where Dave and Bill and Brian drank up most of their profit, and then bought a case of DB Beer to bring home.

The next day Brian and I went to work. We worked for three more days, and walked away with more than $50 each, which was more money than either of us had seen in one place in months. We paid the rent, and I bought a green corduroy shirt for four dollars, a can of beef stew, and a case of DBs. Brian stashed his cash under his mattress, went to bed early each night, and to everyone's surprise, worked all the next day, which made it an entire week.

It was Friday night, and Ian, a surfer who lived up the road from us, was going into Coolangatta, to a pub called *The Cabbage Patch*. He asked us to go along. I ironed my best Levis with a hot water bottle and put on my new shirt. The others pulled out their best shirts and pants from the bottoms of cardboard boxes.

Dave cast an envious eye on my shirt as we entered Ian's Holden and headed out to the Patch. Having been away from women for so long, the boys were a little awkward until they had a few beers in them. Brian was the first to make a move. He asked twin sisters, who's eyes were painted with big, white stars around them, to dance. Bill danced alone, shyly by the jute box. Dave found a nice woman to dance with, but let go of her when her husband arrived. I sat alone at the table until a cute girl with straight blond hair asked me to dance with her. We got to talking and she was intrigued by me being American. I introduced her to Dave. He kissed her hand, and turned to me saying, "Damn capitalist," as he pulled at the corduroy shirt in anger. I had never seen him like this before, and figured that it was the alcohol.

The girl's name was Karen and I asked Ian if we could drop her off at her house, which was on the way back to Byron. "No worries mate," he said. Dave grabbed the keys from Ian and got into the driver's seat. He started the car, and drove down the dark road, back toward the Ark. I sat in the back seat, talking quietly to Karen. Dave had one arm on the wheel and pressed the other onto the car seat. He kept looking back to see what I was doing. I warned him repeatedly against on-coming traffic, and he mumbled something about my new shirt, before turning around again. Just as Dave was turning back around, I reached over to kiss Karen on the cheek.

It was not so much a crash as a loud thud. The left-front fender and the tree had become one. Karen was crying in my arms, and Dave, who sat in the front seat with the engine still running, looked to me and said, as if it were my fault, "Well, Matie, I just hit a tree."

Just as Brian had become a slave to the promise he made to Officer Shales, so now Dave was a slave to Ian, who wanted his car repaired. At first Dave and Brian worked every day, while Bill and I surfed and fished. Within a week, however, Bill and I became bored with one another, and so we went to work ourselves. Within a month, Dave had paid off his debt to Ian. That was the very day that Dave quit work.

We all tried to act as if nothing had happened and attempted to return to the old ways of the Ark. But it could never be. Bill and Brian had discovered things like watches and clocks and flannel pajamas, and spent all of their time working. Dave said that there was no turning back for them.

I worked for a solid month, and missed one of the best winter swells ever to hit Byron Bay. Dave and Bill, who hung out together more and more often, would tell us about endless six-foot waves. Brian worked full-time and then spent his free time with Officer Shales. I had become very lonely.

"Dave, what's become of the Ark?" I asked, one evening as we sat together in the tall grass overlooking the surf while he smoked a hand-rolled cigarette.

"I told you once that you were becoming a damn capitalist. It was the shirt that started it. You know you never would have gotten that girl if you hadn't been wearing that green shirt, don't you mate? Ah, it's a shame to see that you went that way. Now you've infected Brian also."

I had never admired anyone as much as I did Dave, and his words cut deeply. I walked out in the fading light, to the point where I sat alone, remembering my narrow escape in the caravan a few months earlier, and watching the whitewater of the waves peel perfectly along the sandbar. I contemplated the things that were dear to me, and then I knew that Dave was right.

When I returned to the Ark, I reached into my pack, pulled out my green shirt, and offered it to Dave. He put his hands upon my shoulders, looked me squarely in the eyes and took the shirt to the woodstove where he triumphantly tossed it into the fire.

Brian was seated at the kitchen table, reading a pamphlet about the Police Academy in Sydney. Without apology, he told me that he was moving out of the Ark, and applying to the police academy. I wished him well and then went to my corner of the house where I lay awake, looking up at the wooden ceiling, feeling very much alone.

The next day I awoke early, and walked out to see that a new swell had hit Byron Bay. Lines poured in evenly and peeled with power down the point.

For the first time in months the four of us surfed together, riding waves deep in the pocket for hundreds of yards. That evening at home, Brian officially revealed his plan to become a police officer to all of us. It was evident that there was no changing his mind. The next day Dave told me about the party we were going to have for Brian.

I took all of my money from the bank and went to the meat works to buy half a pig. Then Bill and I went into the frontyard to pick all of the corn. We ordered a keg from the pub. I bought Brian a card and a green corduroy shirt, and tucked my remaining ten dollars into a pocket in his pack.

The night before the party, we dug a pit and placed the pig in it. The corn was roasted. The keg was tapped, and we cleaned and decorated the Ark with colored paper. A local rock band played. There had never been such a party in Byron Bay. Surfers drove up from Noosa. Girls, including Karen, came from as far away as Coolangatta. Hippies came out of their communes. Even Officer Shales and his wife arrived to eat and drink and dance in honor of Brian, who had the first dance with Mrs. Shales.

Brian rotated partners, and eventually settled in with Karen. He was wearing the green corduroy shirt that I had given him, and I had to admit that Dave was right as usual. Dave, who could see that I was a bit hurt by losing Karen, walked up and handed me a beer. He motioned to where Karen and Brian were dancing and said, "She goes good with the flat-top, don't she?" By midnight we had eaten all of the food, and drank all of the beer. Ian went home and returned with three gallons of wine. The party continued until dawn, and sprawled out for two more days. People pitched tents near the Ark and we feasted on fish, and surfed and played guitars under the stars, watching the waves and

163

telling lies about the big surf we had ridden.

Gradually, in about a month, everybody went home. Things soon returned to normal, getting good waves, catching fish, and drinking wine whenever we had any. We missed Brian, but he wrote to say that he was at the top of his class. And every so often Dave would call a meeting, and sadly announce that there was a crisis. Then one of us would go to work for about a week, being cautious not to fall for the evils of capitalism again.

Just before I left the Ark and Australia to return to the States, a bewildered young man stumbled upon the house and asked for a place to stay. Dave put his arm on the lad's shoulder, welcomed him in his saintly fashion and told him to keep the doors closed when he went away. You never knew when some confused old goat might wander in, remembering that it had once been his home a long time ago.

*What kind of man is this? Even the winds and the waves obey him!"*

—Matthew 8: 27

# GOOD THINGS LOVE WATER

To Order *GOOD THINGS LOVE WATER*

Please send $17.95 check or money order, to:

Chubasco Publishing Company
P.O. Box 697
Cardiff-by-the-Sea, CA 92007

The price includes tax, postage and handling.

# GOOD THINGS LOVE WATER